Hour Power

HOUR POWER

John W. Lee

With Milton Pierce

DJ-I **DOW JONES-IRWIN** Homewood, Illinois 60430

ISBN 0-87094-186-0
Library of Congress Catalog Card No.80-70146
Printed in the United States of America

1234567890D76543210

Contents

Introduction

Be not as one that hath ten thousand years to live; death is nigh at hand; while thou livest, while thou hast time, be good.

— Marcus Aurelius

A few years ago, I was asked to address a very unusual group of people on the subject of time management. The group is called Make Today Count, and its members are unique. They are all dying, suffering from a terminal illness.

At one point, I asked the group to write down what they thought people would remember them for most. As they were writing, I told them that people tend to remember others for their accomplishments. Your achievements outlast you and cause others to recall you from time to time. If your accomplishments are great enough, you are remembered throughout history.

When I read their answers, however, the group showed me I was wrong. Above all else, they said, people will remember how you treated them. If you were kind, sharing, giving to them, people will remember this. People will remember your personal style.

7

They were absolutely correct. I've been around for a while now, and I've lost several friends and relatives over the years. And when I think back and remember them, I don't recall the fact that they made a lot of money, or that they were exceptional in their field of work. I remember their style. The way they laughed, or talked, or how they helped me in a time of trouble or confusion.

You, too, will be remembered for your style. *Unfortunately, many people are so busy trying to catch up with their own responsibilities that they have no time for style, no time to be kind, courteous and considerate.*

This illustration should point out to you the focus of this book: discovering more efficient ways to accomplish your goals is more than just finding shortcuts. It's developing a whole style of life that allows you more time for creating relationships, for building your own sense of achievement, for making yourself and others just a little bit better.

There is something called the "Activity Trap," and most of us fall into it now and then. We get so wrapped up in our pursuit of success — whether working overtime, building up a new business, or whatever — that we forget to balance our lives. Success and happiness are not one-dimensional things. Success at work alone does not bring happiness, as lots of lonely executives can tell you. Nor does the love of someone we care for fulfill us completely. There must be a balance between achievement and emotion and between work and free time pursuits that will bring a total joy into our lives.

The new efficiency you develop at work should lead to greater success in that aspect of your life. And, with the time you save, you will be free to share more of your life and personality with those you love. From the balance of these factors: efficiency, success, and style — comes the real happiness of life. You will not only do well at work, but you will also have time to give to your family and friends. You will have success and style at the same time, through one program of time saving.

The problem confronting us all is not too little time, but too little imagination in utilizing the time we have. The how-to sections of this book can show you how to accomplish more and gain more satisfaction in nearly every aspect of your life — your career, your leisure, even the unavoidable chores of daily living. You can actually accomplish 50 percent more in your waking hours than you are right now. It's easy, provided you get serious about Hour Power.

Hour Power is the mastery of time. It is the ability to make the most of every minute, every hour, and every day. It is a zest for life . . . an enjoyment of the moment . . . the ability to take charge of your life and make things happen — not by accident or chance, but by design.

In my lectures I frequently ask for a show of hands from the men and women in the audience to see how many have a good idea of where they're going to be, say, four or five years from today. Once I posed that question before a gathering of nearly 200 people in Tallahassee, Florida. Out of the entire audience only *one* hand went up. I walked over to the neatly dressed young man and asked him what made him different from so many of the rest of us, what had given him the self-discipline to map out a course for himself, while others are content to just let their lives drift.

"Dr. Lee," he said, "you don't understand. You see, I'm an inmate in the Florida State Correctional Facility near here and I'm attending this lecture on a special pass as part of an in-prison degree program. So I know exactly where I'll be for the next ten years until I come up for parole!"

Regrettably, few of us bother to plan ahead for more than a few weeks or months at a time, unless plans are forced on us. It has been said that "Most people are too busy earning a living to make any money." To put it another way: "People concentrate so entirely on day-to-day problems that they don't make plans and take the initiatives they should to really get ahead.

That observation applies equally well to all aspects of our lives and not just to the problem of earning a living. It's a rare individual who thinks seriously and methodically about the future of his family life, his intellectual development, his own place in the community. Maybe that's why so many of our dreams go unrealized.

The principal benefit of Hour Power is that it gives you time for your family and friends and time for yourself. It will help you avoid the activity trap! Most of the time-saving samples I use relate to office work, but the principles can be applied to any type of job — including homemaking. The first step is to take inventory of your goals and objectives. Let's begin that process now.

1

Whys Before Hows

Thy purpose firm is equal to the deed...

— Edward Young

Hour Power is a system of living that is designed to help you get what you want from life, whatever it may be. But first, you must decide what your goals are. You must ask yourself: "What do I want from life?" and "Why?"

No matter what your goal is, my Hour Power system will help you attain any goal or desire whatsoever. The nature of your goals is unimportant. What matters most is that you be able to define them. For until you can state what you want in life in one simple sentence, you will be working toward nothing.

I've entitled this chapter "Whys before Hows" because I believe that this phrase is the key to success with my program. Most people invest in a book like this because they want to know HOW: How to make more money . . . how to have more leisure time . . . how to succeed.

But before you can begin to consider HOW to get what you want, you must know WHY you want it. You have to stop and examine where your life is going today, where you'd like to be tomorrow, or next month, or next year. You should even consider exactly what you want to accomplish before you die.

Determining your WHYs in life is really very simple. To accomplish it, you will use a system called "Values Clarification." It's an easy way to decide what things in life have meaning and importance to you — what things you consider worth working for.

Like some of the other ideas in this book, Values Clarification is not revolutionary. But my way of using it is.

You've probably read many articles about learning to get more from life, and every one of them has probably asked you to write down your ultimate goals. And chances are, you didn't bother. Maybe it reminded you of sitting in grammar school and having your teacher ask you to write down what you want to be when you grow up. Or maybe you just thought the whole idea was too childish, embarrassing, or open-ended to have meaning.

I have a radical idea that I think will pull you out of your complacency. It's an exercise in creative writing. I want you to write your own obituary.

Exercise 1: Imagine that you passed away quietly during the night, without pain or struggle. The next day, every paper in the state is running an obituary describing your life, complete with a banner headline. What might this remembrance have to say?

The following is your obituary, without any of the essential details. It's up to you to fill these details in. And feel free to be imaginative. Let your fantasy run free. Plug in the facts that would make your life seem happy and successful beyond your wildest dreams.

First, you'll need some paper and a pencil. And then, you'll need some creativity.

Don't rush this exercise. If you want to take some time to think about it, put the book down and don't read any further until your obituary is complete.

Here's the basic outline:

Write Your Own Obituary

_____, of _____,
(Mr. Mrs. Ms.) name   (your dream address)

died last night at the age of _____. (He, She) spent over

_____ years in the field of _____,

where he/she rose to the position of _____.

But beyond this work, (he, she) is probably best known for _____

_____

Among_____'s most favored and successful
(Mr. Mrs. Ms.)

interests were   _____, _____

and _____.

(He, She) was also a renowned _____.

_____ is survived by
(Mr. Mrs. Ms.)

_____ and _____.

The estate is estimated at _____.

When your obituary is completed, go back and take a look at
it. If you performed this exercise correctly, it should describe a
life so full, so complete that anyone would love to have lived it.
Your obituary should show that you have accomplished all your
desires, reached all your goals, and, having nothing left to do,
died gracefully and with a feeling of fulfillment.

Your obituary is probably unique, unlike anyone else's. Your
dream address might be a manor house in the suburbs, a pent-
house suite in midtown, or a beachfront home in Bermuda.
Your field of endeavor could be business, music, law, or any

other form of human work. You might have risen to the position of chairman of the board, Nobel Prize winner, or king. Your other pursuits could have included searching for a cure for cancer, painting or writing, handywork, athletics or any other hobby or interest. Your survivors might be numerous, and your estate could have been worth billions.

It doesn't matter what details you put in the basic obituary. What matters is the reason you chose a certain career or interest over all the others available. Your choice reflects your goals in life. Of course, you've probably built your dream life up beyond what you actually expect to achieve before you die.

For now, let's use this obituary as a source of your goals in life. I'd like you to look at each entry you made and ask yourself "Why would I want that?" Again, a little paper work is needed.

Write down each of the details you entered in your obituary, and next to it state the reason why you made this choice. Be as specific and honest as possible. Even if the answer is "I don't know why," write that down, too.

Your list may look something like the one opposite.

We are now beginning to understand the WHY of your life. You have just seen what you would like your life to be if you had three magic wishes. Now, let's turn our creativity to the problems you have right now — today — and how you view them.

I have another slightly depressing exercise for you to do. Try to imagine that you have exactly 24 hours to live. At this very moment tomorrow, you will be dead. There is no chance involved, no way to escape, no alternative. Twenty-four hours and it's all over.

What would you do? Would you sleep tonight? Go to work tomorrow? Run to the nearest church and start praying?

Exercise 2: I'd like you to make a list of everything you would and would not do in the last 24 hours of your life. Start with

Reasons for Life Goals

GOAL	WHY
Beach-front home	Because I love the sun and the sea, and would love to retire to Bermuda.
Die at 85	Because I don't want to continue living after I lose my health.
45 years in sales	Because I love selling, I'm good at my job, and I want to work a long time.
Vice President	Because I deserve it, especially the money and prestige.
Known for his parties.......	Because I love people, cherish my friends, and like to entertain them.
Interests were: Golf Cooking Sports	Because I enjoy these more than any other hobbies or pastimes.
Renowned for wealth	Because I'd like to be rich.
Survived by wife/husband, three children	I am happily married, have two children, and I would like to have one more.
Estate: $1,000,000	Because I want to provide for my family, but would not save any more than this. I would have spent the rest before I died.

this very moment, and account for every hour you have left.

Your list should consist of three columns: the first listing things you would do; the second listing things you would not do; the third explaining your reasons for choosing what you would do.

Try to imagine that you are actually in this tragic situation. Do not be as fantasy-oriented as you were with your obituary. Instead, give yourself a plan for 24 hours that you could actually use in such a crisis.

When your list is complete, take a good, long look at it. What did you do during those last hours of your life? Did you close out the bank account and head for the nearest massage parlor? Did you take out a new insurance policy for your family's future? Maybe you told the boss what you really think of him, or finally punched that departmental chairman you've always hated.

Let's take a look at an imaginary last-day list (opposite). I'll also include some WHYs, just as you did on your obituary.

If you've taken this second exercise seriously, it should reveal a lot to you about your goals in life. What you have done is to isolate those things that mean the most to you, as well as those that mean nothing at all.

Death has been our topic in both these lists. And this is appropriate. For death is the end of the road for all of us. We will all die eventually. And living life to the fullest really means knowing what you want to do before you die.

Of course, these two exercises have dealt with completely hypothetical situations. But they have a lot to tell us. You have listed your ultimate, long-term goals in life: your fantasy world come true. And you have also decided what elements of your life right now are most important to you.

The key is to compare these lists. How are they different? If in your obituary you gave Bermuda as your address, why didn't you decide to fly south in your last 24 hours? And if you imagined yourself as vice president of sales, why didn't you spend your last day at the job you claim to enjoy?

These two exercises may have shown you the conflicts in your

Last-Day Activities List

THINGS TO DO	*WHY*
Rewrite my will	To insure my family's security.
Call my friends	Because I'd want to talk with the people I love one last time.
Spend the entire 24 hours with my family	Because they are my most treasured gift in this life.
Write a goodbye letter	To say all the things I've never been able to express.

THINGS NOT TO DO	*WHY*
Go to work	Who cares now?
Sleep	I haven't the time.
Watch T.V.	A total waste of my energy.
Argue	My life is too short for this.

own goals. If so, then they have worked. Don't feel you've failed a test: we all have great conflicts of purpose. In the long run, we know we must work for security, stability, and respect. But with one day left to live, these factors may take second place to more emotional goals.

Sometime between the distant future and today, your goals can be found. They are probably a combination of career responsibilities and personal pleasure . . . monetary needs and emotional desires. Life is conflict, and your goals are no exception. But finding that happy middle-ground, defining it as accurately as possible, and feeling comfortable with it will be your path to success.

Consider the conflicting goals you live with every day. Surely none of us would list "watching lots of TV" as a life objective. And yet, we do exactly that every day.

I'm not saying you should give up watching TV. We all need to relax and stop thinking sometimes. But if you consider long-term and immediate goals as actually being the same thing, operating together, you may find it easier to create useful, attainable goals for yourself.

That obituary will be written someday. It's as certain as the rising sun. Will it sound like the one you've written? When will it come? Tomorrow? Next year?

Of course, you can't live as if this was your last day. Nor should you simply point yourself toward those goals for the distant future. The answer is to find a middle-ground, a system of goals that will work for today and for the years to come.

If you've done these two exercises, then you are now ready to define those goals. And this time, there won't be as many restrictions on you.

I've broken down your goals into four categories: career, finances, personal growth, and emotion. These four categories include just about every aspect of life. And it's important for you to have a well-defined goal for each area.

Exercise 3: Under each category, I'd like you to state a goal for three separate periods: today, five years from now, and ten years from now. This is the way to find your one goal for all the phases of your life. By first knowing what you want at each point in the future, you can discover what you want from your life as a whole. And you can form the goals that will help you get whatever you want.

Your goal list should like the one on the opposite page.

Before you fill in this chart, go back and reread your obituary and last-day plan. Ask yourself why those two exercises turned out as they did. Re-examine your own motives and

List of Goals

Career:
    Today: _____
    Five Years: _____
    Ten Years: _____

Finances:
    Today: _____
    Five Years: _____
    Ten Years: _____

Personal Growth:
    Today: _____
    Five Years: _____
    Ten Years: _____

Emotional:
    Today: _____
    Five Years: _____
    Ten Years: _____

feelings. The secret to forming good goals lies in self-examination.

When you do this third exercise, take your time. Consider every entry carefully, as though you were filling out your tax return. Rewrite your chart as many times as you feel necessary. Do a thorough, careful job.

Stop and fill out the chart. Read no further until it is finished.

When you've completed this list, you've learned a lot about yourself. You've put aside all the daily problems that bother you and take up your energy, and replaced them with a clear concise list of what you truly consider important in life.

Forming one perfect goal for your life is a matter of taking the time-coded objectives you just listed and finding the one factor that unifies them. For within each of these goals, there is a simple concern that links them together. This concept is your life's goal.

Let's look at a sample chart. It may read like this:

Career:

Today: Get more done than yesterday. Create a new system for higher productivity. Stop wasting time.

Five Years: To be named Vice-President. To do more important work. To be highly respected in my field.

Ten Years: My own business. Profits coming in each day. Retirement a possibility I can choose at any time.

If you look at the three entries in this chart, a simple common denominator emerges. This person wants to work better toward the goal of independence, success, and respect. Each of the stages he has described shows a growth in these qualities.

Independence, success and respect in a career is a good goal. But it is not yet a WHY. It does not tell us WHY this person wants to attain these goals.

If asked why, our fictitious person might say: "I want to work better because I desire independence, success and respect." This person had stated in one sentence not only what he wants from life, but also how he intends to get it. With a WHY goal like this, the Hour Power system will enable this person to attain what he (or she) desires most.

Let's move on to the next category: finances. Our sample chart looks like this:

Finances:

    Today: Cut back on one expense. Put savings in the bank.

    Five Years: Have made successful stock investments that will bring big profits.

    Ten Years: Have my total value quadruple. Stocks are steady, some are growing. Dividends pay my monthly bills.

This person's financial goals are clear. Like everyone, he wants more money. And he plans to use methods of saving and investing to attain this goal.

Turning this into a WHY goal is easy: "I want to save and invest wisely because I desire financial security and more money."

The WHY goal may not sound very different from other statements. But it shows you in one sentence both the final desired outcome and the path to it. It is a complete concept for building toward the future — or even just toward tomorrow.

This WHY goal makes as much sense and has as much to say in the immediate future as it will in years to come. It is at once a declaration of your intentions to fight for what you want, and will also serve as a reminder to you in times of weakness or temptation.

I suggest you go through your time-coded chart and form simple WHY goals. Write them down, some place where they will never be lost. It might even be a good idea to frame them and hang them where you can't help but notice them every day.

In all, you will have four WHY goals to live your life by, one for each of the four major areas of our experience: career, finances, personal growth and emotions.

Your four goals may sound like this:

Career:	"I want to perfect my working system so I can have a higher income, a better position, and a more interesting career."
Finances:	"I want to control my spending and saving so I can have more of the material things I want in the future."
Personal Growth:	"I want to read more and keep better informed so I can get more out of life and give more to my children."
Emotions:	"I want to keep open communication and closeness with my family so we can learn to love and respect each other more each year."

Or, your goals may be completely different from these. It really doesn't matter. The nature of your goal is not important. What is crucial, though, is that you understand your own goals. Without understanding them you cannot begin to improve your life.

But once you know the WHY, the HOW comes more easily; you can use the techniques and ideas in this book to make of your life exactly what you wish.

It is essential that you do not proceed with this program until you are quite certain of your goals. It is a good idea to go back and rethink all three of the exercises we've done so far. Ask yourself again if your answers were honest and revealing enough. Reconsider what objectives you listed for five and ten years from now.

Again, self-examination is the secret. Do not hesitate to completely redo these exercises, perhaps over and over again, if it will lead you to more truthful answers.

However, there will also be many times when different goals are each competing for your attention. Work may interfere with family life. Thriftiness may conflict with your desire to give your children everything they want. Your struggle for personal growth may directly interfere with other considerations, like household chores.

When these scheduling conflicts occur, you will need to establish priorities: one goal will have to come first. Hour Power gives you an excellent system for setting your priorities. It allows you to pursue one goal at a time, without sacrificing anything from your other objectives and desires. This system of priorities is outlined and explained in the next chapter.

One final factor to keep in mind is that in time, your goals may change. You know that today you do not desire or work for the same things you wanted in high school or college. In the same way, ten years from now your goals may be quite different.

Psychologists have shown us how a developing person goes through many distinct stages on the road to adulthood. But what most people don't realize is that adulthood, too, is a series of stages. Every few years, we change in many important ways. And our system of goals must be flexible enough to change with us.

Clearly, the objectives of a person of 25 will be quite distinct from the dreams and desires of a person sixty. But, at any age, knowledge and understanding of your own goals is absolutely essential.

As the years go by, be sure to review your goals. Chances are, they will need changing and updating. And this review will also give you a chance to see how far you've come, how much progress you've made, and what exactly you've achieved.

Your firm purpose is equal to the deed. With a good system of values and goals, you are ready to go to work. You are ready to change your life.

The WHYs are out of our way now. Let's get on to the HOWs.

2

Establishing Priorities

Pay attention to matters of importance.

— Diogenes Laertius

Defining the term "priority" is a simple task: priority is choice. Every time you choose to do one thing before another, you are establishing priorities in your life. Shower before you get dressed. Eat the entrée before the dessert. Take a nap before you paint the garage. Cook dinner before you do the dishes.

A choice is made, and in so doing, a priority is established. One activity has been assigned greater importance than another.

If miracles could be made to happen on demand, most of us would like to be rich and idle. Of course, we would have to be rich first and idle second. Even our fantasies have certain priorities.

But there's a conflict of ideas here. You don't get rich by being idle. This is a perfect example of goals and choices in opposition. Your goal in this life may be wealth, and yet you would not actively choose to do the work that leads to success. Given your druthers, you'd be more likely to choose television.

But success doesn't come that way. Goals are achieved by people who choose to work for them. Your number one priority should be to perform those tasks that will lead you to your goal.

How can you form priorities . . . for today, for the future?

How do you assign different levels of priority? What do you do when two priorities conflict?

The answer can be found in what I call the "Objective Activity Time System." It's a way of knowing what you're doing with your time, what goals you're working toward, and when you are wasting time.

Your individual priorities come directly from your goals. So you must return to these goals before you can establish your priorities and choose your actions. But first, let's talk about objective activity.

Every moment of your life you are involved in some form of activity. Even sleeping is activity. And each and every one of these actions is chosen, even the ones you think you do because you have to.

So you make choices, take actions . . . isn't that establishing priorities? It most certainly is. But why, then, aren't you reaching your goals?

Because you aren't choosing to work toward your goals. You don't know for sure what you're working toward. You simply don't know what you're doing.

Most people find it almost impossible to be objective about their own actions. All day long, they do things, work hard, try to concentrate. But they don't relate these activities to goals. They don't have an objective, organized, common sense understanding of how today's work relates to tomorrow, next week, or next year.

The Objective Activity Time System gives you a way to understand your own behavior. The secret is to look backwards from your goals instead of forward from your actions. With Objective Activity, your goals become part of your everyday life. They set your priorities and determine what you will do, and when you will do it.

Go back to the last chapter and find those four goals you decided on. (They actually should be locked in your memory, or framed on your wall.) For the sake of example, we'll use four hypothetical goals that might be a lot like your own.

Career:	"I want to work better because I want success and respect."
Finance:	"I want to save and invest wisely because I desire security and independence."
Personal:	"I want to study and expand my skills so I can get more from life."
Emotions:	"I want to be a good spouse and parent and share myself with others."

Imagine for a moment that you can choose only one of your goals. Which would it be? Career? Emotion? Growth? Which one of these different areas of life means the most to you?

It's an impossible question to answer. And yet, you are constantly forced to choose one goal over another. When you go to work, you are placing one goal above the rest. When you decide to take a day off and be with your children, you're choosing another goal.

Without clear priorities, you cannot make these choices as best you should. You may select the wrong goal at the wrong time. And since your priorities may be constantly shifting, it is likely that without priorities you will move from an important activity to a meaningless one. You may waste half of your life on work that leads nowhere.

Listen to this story I heard recently. I think it says something about priorities.

An elderly widow has decided to spend a week or two in Miami Beach. This is her only chance to get away from the northern snows for a while, and she's looking forward to it. But she has one problem: she doesn't like to travel alone.

She thinks it might be a nice idea to bring her grandson along. The boy is 11 years old, and would probably like the trip. But there's one problem. The boy is her daughter's only child, and the young mother and her husband are fiercely protective of their son. To say the least, he is their prized possession.

The grandmother asks her daughter if the boy can come along to Miami Beach. At first, the daughter says no, claiming the woman is too old to care for him and protect him from harm. But after lots of prodding and reassurances, the daughter agrees, and the boy begins packing for his trip.

Soon, the old lady and her grandson arrive at Miami Beach. The boy is very well behaved, and looks surprisingly calm in his little blue suit and blue cap. The grandmother suggests that even before they check into the hotel, they go down and look at the ocean.

This unusual couple stands at the edge of the shore, an old woman in old-fashioned clothes and a young boy in a blue suit and cap. They look out with joy at the lovely Atlantic Ocean.

Suddenly, the sea roars, the wind howls, and a giant wave reaches up onto the shore, grabbing the little boy and dragging him into the ocean's depths. When the wave is gone, the old woman can find no trace of her grandson.

She turns her gaze toward heaven, thinking of her only daughter's only son, gone! Gone for good! She begs God to help her.

"Please, God!" she cries. "Please give me my grandson back. I beg you, God, just let him come back, and I'll never ask you for anything else as long as I live."

Suddenly, the sea roars again, the wind howls, and another wave, as tremendous as the first, replaces the little boy where he stood before.

The old lady looks down at the little boy, who again stands quietly in his little blue suit. She looks at him long and hard, then turns her eyes back toward heaven and says, "He had a hat."

Like most people, this woman has a problem with priorities. She recognized a crisis when it happened, but once it was passed, she returned to trivial things. Did she call an ambulance? Check for injuries? No. She wanted the child's hat!

In your life, the same priority problem is wasting your time. You do one job, work hard at it, and then when it's done, you say, "Good! Now I can waste time." If you had an objective view of your own actions, you would have a second priority waiting when that first important project was completed.

Importance is what priority is all about. If your priorities are right, you will choose your activities in descending order of importance.

For most people, the four major life goals (mentioned earlier in this chapter) are deeply interconnected. Achieving your career goal will help you attain your financial goal. If you reach your goal in personal growth, you will be a better and more interesting person, which should help in your career. And the success you find in your career and finances will let you achieve your emotional goal.

But at different times of the day, or on different days of the week, one goal must take priority over the others. It is this day-to-day setting and juggling of priorities that Objective Activity Time System is concerned with.

First, I want you to create a chart outlining the different sequences in your average work-day. The sample chart on the next page can be modified to show your actual schedule (no matter what your occupation).

Now assign a goal (Career, Finances, Personal Growth, or Emotional) to each part of your day, making that goal the number one priority for that time period.

Let's begin with the hours before you arrive at work, or before you begin your daily chores.

Average Workday Chart

Before Work:

6:30 – 8:00 _____

8:00 – 9:00 _____

Work:

9:00 – 12:00 _____

1:00 – 5:00 _____

After Work:

5:00 – 6:00 _____

6:00 – 7:00 _____

7:00 – Bed _____

Before Work:

6:00 – 8:00 _____

8:00 – 9:00 _____

From 6:30, when you awake, until 8:00 when you leave for work, you are largely occupied with getting ready for the day. Washing, dressing, eating, etc. These activities, when viewed objectively, are part of your career goal. You are preparing yourself to work. So you can assign "Career" to this time.

6:30 – 8:00 — Career

But wait! You also have an opportunity during this time to talk with your family, listen to their problems, discuss their interests. You can use some of this time to share yourself with those you love. So why not give this time to the fourth goal — Emotional?

Consider this objectively. It would be nice, if while getting ready for work, you could spend a little time with your family. But if you don't get out the door on time, you'll arrive late for work. Which is more important?

You haven't even left the house yet, and already you're establishing priorities.

Obviously, one goal has to take a back seat. The decision is yours to make. No one can help you. But for our sample case, I'll choose getting to work on time as the more important activity. So the order of priorities in this time period is:

Before Work:
 6:30 – 8:00 — Career, Emotional

At 8:00, you start your trek to the office. Again, this activity is essentially dedicated to your career goal.

8:00 – 9:00 — Career.

But isn't there something else you could be doing with this time? Reading a book, glancing through the day's newspaper, or just listening to the news on your car radio? Why not include Personal Growth in this time?

Why not indeed! Whenever you can accomplish more than one thing at a time, and do them both well, by all means do so.

But keep in mind that one is more important than the other. Here is the ranking of priorities:

Before Work:
   6:30 - 8:00 — Career, Emotional
   8:00 - 9:00 — Career, Personal Growth

Our example is a simple one, but it illustrates a vital concept. If you have a set of priorities for every hour of the day, you will take the first step toward eliminating wasted time. You can begin to accomplish more than one activity at once. You can start knowing what you're doing.

Once you arrive at work, your number one priority is obvious. Your career goal should constantly be the first thing on your mind during these hours. As clear-cut as that may seem, most people don't really understand it.

How often do you take a break right in the middle of a project — to call a friend, or look at a newspaper or daydream about something besides work? If you're like most people, you get distracted from your career goal as many as 50 times every day.

When you set aside your career goal during working hours, how objective are you being? Do you call home specifically because you want to accomplish two things at once . . . because you want to pursue your emotional goal? Do you really make this kind of conscious decision? Or do you simply call home as a way of breaking the monotony of working?

By setting your level of priorities, you can still call home, balance your checkbook, or do anything at all during work hours and still be objective about pursuing your goals. The trick is to evaluate the importance of each goal and never abandon the first goal until you absolutely must. In other words, set your top priority and stick to it, but have second and third priorities in mind just in case you need them.

Your number one priority during working hours should always be your career goal. If you want to get ahead in your business, or be an efficient homemaker, you must work at it. But what if your broker calls with urgent news about your stock portfolio? Do you stick with your first priority and tell him to leave you alone? Of course not! So the career goal is your first priority, and the finances goal is your second.

But what if your spouse calls and wants to talk about some problem? This might be just as important as your stock broker's call. But remember, you'll have lots of time to discuss family matters tonight. Make the emotional goal your third priority during work hours.

How about Personal Growth? Where does that fit into your work day? Again, the decision is entirely yours. But for my money, personal growth goals should never supersede career goals during a work day. Leave your personal development for your personal time.

Now your priorities for working hours are set:

Work:

9:00 – 12:00 — Career, Finances, Emotional

1:00 – 5:00 — Career, Finances, Emotional

But how do you put this system to work for you? How do you decide when to put your first priority aside to take care of other matters?

This is a question of split-second decision making. The tool that will make it work right is Objective Activity Analysis.

When your first priority is interrupted by a lower priority, you must decide which activity to pursue. You can reach this decision by asking yourself a few simple questions.

Let's imagine your spouse calls during an important meeting. Your priorities immediately tell you not even to take the call. You ask your secretary to tell your spouse you'll call back. But your spouse says it's an emergency.

It seems the plumber who's working on your kitchen sink needs some information. Should you temporarily adjourn your business meeting and speak with the plumber?

That sink affects both your emotional goal and your financial goal. But is it important enough to take away from your first priority, your career?

Ask yourself these questions:

1. Is this activity going to bring me closer to any of my goals?
2. Which activity will bring more goal-success?
3. Can I shift priorities without wasting time?

For our example, the first question would be answered 'yes.' Getting that sink in good working order will help your family and also protects your major investment — your home. It therefore brings you closer to two of your life goals.

Question 2 is a little more difficult to answer. The sink is important, but this business meeting is absolutely urgent. If you handle it right, this meeting might lead to a promotion. The answer to question 2 is "This meeting will bring more goal success."

Question 3 can be answered only with an emphatic "NO!" At this point, it becomes clear what you should do: Have your secretary tell your spouse to let the plumber handle it.

Question 3 could have been answered with a "yes" if the two activities had been virtually equal in goal-success values. Let's say the meeting really wasn't very important, just about equal in urgency to the phone call. In that case, you should talk to your spouse about the sink then continue the meeting.

Problems like this will come up constantly. They even occur within one priority level. During many business days, you will be forced to choose one project over another, and you may often wonder which job is more important. Again, use the three Objective Activity Analysis questions:

1. Is this activity going to bring me closer to any of my goals?
2. Which activity will bring more goal-success?
3. Can I shift priorities without wasting time?

From these three questions, you will gain enough objective information to make a solid decision, and move that much closer toward attaining your goal.

When you have first, second, and third priorities for every waking hour, you are in a position to make the absolute most of your time — for the minute priority number one is satisfied, you are ready to move on to priority number two, and then number three. You are prepared to get things done.

After work, your time will be largely devoted to relaxing and talking with your family. Personal growth and emotional goals will be your first and second priorities here. But again, career or financial matters may cross over into your personal time. Give these areas a lower priority, but be ready to shift if you must.

When deciding what to do during your personal time, you should again use the three Objective Activity Analysis questions. Deciding what goal an activity relates to, which activity will bring the most success, and how much time-wasting a shift will necessitate, will tell you what action to take.

Go back now to the chart for your working day. Assign a first priority to each time slot, and also list any second or third priorities you think apply. Along with your four goals, this schedule should always be kept handy. It is the basic building-block for your Hour Power Time Management program.

Later in this book, I'll talk about the importance of thinking and planning. In thinking and planning, you will use your basic daily schedule to decide what exact projects should be given what level of priority.

For now, let's take our exercise one simple step further. Think about the specific activities you have planned for tomorrow, and give them each a level of priority in your day. Perhaps your son has a test tomorrow in some subject he does not particularly excel in. You may want to talk to him about it tomorrow before work.

Before Work:

    6:30 - 8:00 — Career (get ready)

                — Emotional (talk to Bob about test)

You usually read the paper on the way to work. But a friend just gave you a magazine article that fascinates you. Which should you read? Ask the three Analysis questions. Chances are the article will lead more directly toward your goal of Personal Growth.

    8:00 - 9:00 — Career (get to work)

                — Personal Growth (read that article)

Now we get to the hard part. You're working on three separate accounts this week. They all seem equally important to you, so it's hard to set priority levels. Again, ask the three questions.

By the time you get to the second question you recall your boss mentioning his special interest in one of those projects you're working on. Getting that project done first would not only be an accomplishment, it would be likely to please your boss as well. Give that job top priority.

But what happens if you're interrupted while working on that project? Will you put it aside for a moment? Or will you refuse to acknowledge the interruption? Objective Activity Analysis will give you the answer.

Interruptions and priority shifts like this occur to active people constantly. Recently, I made a study of a few of the top executives I have personally consulted concerning time management. I asked them about interruptions, activity shifts, and many projects going on simultaneously. The average in one day looked like this:

Interruptions: (Telephone, co-workers, etc.)
     87 per day
Activity Shifts: (Changes in project you're working on)
     23 per day
Projects Going on Simultaneously:
     27 per day

With this kind of constant work and activity barrage, a solid priority system is absolutely essential. And if you want this system to work well, it can't be intuitive, or free-floating. It must be written down on paper, analyzed and constantly updated.

Maybe you don't have these kinds of decisions to make every day. But with the new success my Hour Power Program brings you, your schedule may get this hectic sooner than you think.

Define your goals. Set your priorities, and stick to them. Make those three Activity Analysis questions part of your daily thought patterns.

What might you gain from a good system of priorities? Among many benefits, you will find yourself working better because you will know what you're working for. Your goals and your activities will be directly linked, so there will no longer be the overwhelming sense of pointlessness many people feel today.

You will also begin to develop a new kind of flexibility, a way of shifting projects, handling more jobs than one at the same time, and overlapping your four areas of activity without confusion, back-tracking, or wasted time.

And even if the only benefit that comes from using your priority system is that you know what project you should start when another finishes, you will be saving time. If you spend even just ten minutes a day DECIDING what to do next, you are wasting about two full days each year. How much are two days worth to you?

Pay attention to matters of importance. It's a simple system that brings big rewards.

3

Put Time on Your Side!

Backward, turn backward O Time, in your flight, And tell me just one thing I studied last night.

— Anon.

How much do you know about time?

All of us carry around a biological clock that exercises more control than we realize over our activities and emotions. There are some obvious examples of this psychological timepiece in action: the daily cycle of waking and sleeping, for instance, or a woman's monthly cycle. Increasingly, though, social scientists are discovering that there are many biological rhythms in the human animal that pervade all aspects of our lives.

If you had your choice, you would want a car built on a Wednesday. Why? Because industrial statistics show conclusively that people work better on Wednesday. Productivity is highest. Mistakes are fewest. The worst days in terms of quality and quantity of output are Mondays and Fridays. There are hangovers and absenteeisms to contend with on Mondays and also a psychological factor, the Monday morning back-to-work blues. One result: industrial accidents are at their highest on the first day of the work week. Similarly, on Fridays, a "Thank-God-It's Friday" attitude prevails. Workers tend to look forward to the weekend and mistakes start to sneak in.

Here are some other interesting findings:

Medical researchers have determined that blood pressure follows a daily rhythm, dropping to a low point at about 3 a.m. and starting to rise about 5 a.m. The greatest number of heart attacks occur between 6 a.m. and 9 a.m.

According to an article published in the *American Journal of Psychiatry*, there is a striking correlation between the phases of the moon and such extremes of behavior as mental breakdowns and homicides. Crimes increase significantly during the three days immediately after the new and full moon.

Experiments with laboratory animals suggest that it takes fewer drinks to get drunk in the middle of the day than in the hours just before sleep. (A convincing argument against the three-martini lunch?)

Nowadays everyone is familiar with the phenomenon we call "jet lag." When a traveler flies from one time zone to another, his system suffers a shock. On a trip from, say, Tokyo to New York, it may take several days for the traveler to feel rested, refreshed, and capable of peak mental performance. Many corporate executives engaged in sensitive negotiations now routinely schedule some time to recover from jet lag before they begin wheeling and dealing.

Employees who are rotated from one work-shift to another experience a similar array of symptoms. The sudden change in scheduling disrupts their so-called Circadian rhythms — the daily cycles of temperature, blood pressure, and hormonal secretions. In a government-sponsored research program, clinical psychologist Donald Tasto found that working unconventional hours presents "a distinct health hazard." Men and women rotated from one shift to another have a higher incidence of accidents, clinical visits, alcohol use, digestion and sleep problems, as well as dissatisfaction with their personal and domestic lives.

Controversy continues to surround the theory of biorhythms, which has spawned a multi-million dollar-a-year business. There are books on biorhythm, biorhythm newsletters, even biorhythm computers in shopping malls. And for a while the Dallas Cowboys football team employed a firm to prepare weekly biorhythmic cycles, each starting at the moment of birth: a 23-day physical cycle, a 28-day emotional cycle, and a 33-day mental cycle. People are likely to perform well in the up phases of the cycle and poorly in the down or recharging phases. The most vulnerable day comes at the midpoint of each cycle, when a person is changing phases. In a "double critical" day, when two cycles are at midpoint, things are extremely likely to go sour, according to those who believe in this theory. And on a "triple critical" day, when all three cycles are at midpoint — all hell supposedly breaks loose. Mercifully, this occurs only about once a year.

Although this particular, biorhythm theory can no more stand up to scientific scrutiny than astrology or numerology, it doesn't negate legitimate discoveries that have been made about the human biological clock. One fascinating study concerns human sexuality.

When during the day are men at their sexual peak? Do women experience their peak at the same time? Scientists now know for a fact that the male sexual peak is tied to hormone levels and body temperature — and most men are at their erotic best in the early morning. (Now don't say you haven't learned anything useful from this book!) Women also reach their sexual peak early in the morning. Despite this objective biological fact, though, many of us are culturally conditioned to think that the most romantic time of day is the evening. Actually, the hours right before we go to sleep may be the worst time for love-making. Often we're too exhausted emotionally and physically to give or receive the greatest pleasure.

The notion of a peak period of efficiency carries over into our working lives as well. Some people agree with the poet W.H. Auden's line, that "Nothing happens after 9 p.m." Others side with the 9th century Chinese philosopher Lang Chu who states in *The Garden of Pleasures* that "If the day isn't long enough, let's carry our pleasures into the night." Whether you are a night owl or a dawn-driven lark is largely a function of your individual metabolism. If you don't know already, this brief self-test will help you determine when you're at your best. (See *Peak Efficiency Questionnaire* on next page.)

Total up the number of A's and B's. If you have more A's than B's, you're probably a morning person, you do your best work in the A.M. More B's than A's suggest that you're an afternoon or evening person.

The Hour Power system entails synchronizing your work habits with your Circadian rhythms. If you're an afternoon person, don't overload yourself with major tasks from 9 a.m. to noon. However, if you're a Franklinesque early-to-bed, early-to-rise type of person, you would do well to schedule your most difficult task of the working day for the hours immediately after you arrive at work instead of driving yourself to stay up late the night before to finish it. The more energy you waste fighting your natural biological inclinations, the less verve you will bring to the tasks at hand.

If you're a manager — if you have others working under you — you should be aware that there are better and worse times to carry out particular responsibilities. Social-psychological research confirms this. Let's say, for instance, that you have to sit down with some of your employees and straighten them out because they're not doing the job right. Standard practice has been to straighten an employee out — or call him on the carpet — at the end of the day. The thinking is that the employee will

Peak Efficiency Questionnaire

1. Would you rather
   (a) eat a good breakfast in the morning or
   (b) get an extra 15 minutes of sleep?

2. Would you rather play a set of tennis
   (a) before going to work or
   (b) after you get home?

3. Do you need a cup of coffee — or two, or three — to get going?
   (a) No
   (b) Yes

4. Do you sleep late on Saturday and Sunday morning?
   (a) No
   (b) Yes

5. Are you late for work more than twice a month?
   (a) No
   (b) Yes

6. Do you schedule social or entertainment events more than two evenings a week?
   (a) No
   (b) Yes

7. Are you more often surprised to discover it's
   (a) lunch time or
   (b) quitting time?

8. Are you generally awake before your alarm goes off in the morning?
   (a) Yes
   (b) No

then take the problem home that evening and solve it on his own time rather than waste more of the company time. In addition to being rather cynical, this procedure runs counter to an important finding about human nature. We know for a fact that people are at their absolute nastiest just before they eat.

This holds true for animals as well. Play with your cat or dog just before you feed it and see what happens. It is likely to scratch, bite, and otherwise show signs of ill-temper. Taking this one step farther, sociologists have determined that the majority of family fights begin just before dinner. The inescapable conclusion, then, is that the end of the day is the least appropriate time to straighten someone out. Almost inevitably it will lead to sharp exchanges, hard feelings and intensely bitter emotions that might to some extent be avoided if the discussions were carried out at another time of day. Actually, the best time to correct an employee is immediately after lunch when a full stomach can help both parties maintain civility and good spirits.

What's the most favorable time of day to give out a new assignment to a subordinate? Interesting data has been assembled on this question, too. The least effective way to pass out assignments is to pile them on one by one throughout the day. One job at 9:00 a.m., another at 10, and another at 11. Employees get the feeling they're playing Egyptian football. (In my neighborhood we used to call it Egyptian football when someone tried to change the rules of the game while the ball was in the air.) When you load up assignments one after another, an employee feels put upon, picked on. The ideal time to delegate assignments is at the end of the day. When the worker comes into work the next morning, he knows exactly what he has to do and he can set right to work doing it.

By the same token, the best time of day to do some advance planning is also the late afternoon. The reason for this lies in a concept known as "seasoning." If you start planning at 8:30 a.m. for a project you want to start at 9:00 a.m. you have only 30 minutes of seasoning. Not enough! On the other hand, if you put a plan together at 4:30 p.m. — devoting the same 30 minutes of concentrated effort to it — you gain the benefit of maybe 16 hours of seasoning. Consciously or subconsciously, you can refine the plan and improve it. The next day at 9 o'clock you'll have a more mature and better-conceived plan to work with. Seasoning is absolutely fundamental to the execution of a good idea.

Now I'm not saying you should agonize over your plan during dinner, while you're watching television, or when you're trying to get to sleep. Far from it. When you have your plan mapped out before you get in your car and drive home, you can pretty well afford to exclude it from your conscious thoughts. You won't have that nagging feeling that "I really should be preparing for the 9 o'clock meeting." You'll get more sleep, too.

Planning in the afternoon enables you to enjoy what psychologists call "closure." You devote the end of the day to planning and getting organized for the next day, then you can walk away and forget about it. In truth, though, your subconscious mind will continue to elaborate and reformulate your plan in a relaxed and creative spirit. Closure and seasoning are by no means contradictory principles.

All the seasoning in the world, however, will prove futile if the right circumstances are not established. Next, I'll turn your attention to creating the proper conditions for getting things done.

4

The Right Time and Place
for Everything

> *Man is not the creature of circum-*
> *stances. Circumstances are the crea-*
> *tures of men.*
>
> — Benjamin Disraeli

Have you ever been to Las Vegas? If you have, you know how easy it is to lose money in that flamboyant city. As Lenny Bruce once said, they should change the name to "Lost Wages."

Las Vegas casinos are perhaps the best example in this world of creating conditions. The quality, mood, and structure of these places are designed — quite brilliantly, I might add — to almost guarantee that you will gamble. And of course the odds tell us that when you gamble, the house eventually wins.

What's the first thing you see when you walk into a place like Caesar's Palace? Slot machines. You run into them before you find the front desk. And by the time you check in, you've probably lost $20.00.

The clerk then tells you that your room is being cleaned at this very moment. It will be ready in less than half an hour. In the meantime, won't you please have a drink in the bar, compliments of the manager? Guess what you wind up doing while you wait? You gamble. And probably lose another 50 bucks.

Finally, you get to your room, settle in, and then head back downstairs for dinner. As you wait in line for a table, guess what you're standing next to? Right, slot machines. You lose again.

I call it "Las Vegas Engineering." Every detail of the environment has been carefully planned to encourage you to give up your hard-earned cash. Some casinos hire famous sports stars, now past their prime, just to circulate among the gamblers and make them feel at home. Even the location of the city itself seems carefully planned. When it's 110 degrees in the shade, people find it hard to stay out of the nice, air-conditioned gambling rooms.

Can we apply the principles of Las Vegas engineering in a positive way to produce success promoting conditions? I believe we can!

Did you know that just by moving your desk, relocating your filing cabinets, or installing a small refrigerator in your office, you can increase productivity, save time, and thus produce higher profits? It's true. You can create the conditions that encourage success. And at home, the location of your housework tools and the conditions you create determine how many things you accomplish successfully.

If you're feeling a little skeptical about this, you are not alone. Most Americans feel such helplessness and alienation that the idea of controlling their own destinies and living conditions seems like an impossible dream. But if you doubt the effect of conditions on our behavior, listen to this story from *Sports Illustrated:*

While traveling to South Bend, Indiana for a game against Notre Dame, the University of San Francisco basketball team ran into a few problems. First, they were forced to make the long trip by bus because no planes could land in South Bend due to bad weather. The bus broke down mid-way, and the athletes were put on a second vehicle. Many were forced to stand. They arrived in South Bend without luggage and spent the night in a hotel without heat. They slept that night in street clothes, bundling up in any blankets they could find. The temperature outside was 17 degrees. The following day, San Francisco was defeated by Notre Dame, 88-69.

Through effort, planning, and trial and error, some American businesses have discovered ways to create positive working conditions. The changes made vary from minor operational adjustments, to technological advances and even relocation. The state of Idaho, for example, has experienced a tremendous influx of business from the crowded, crime-ridden urban centers of the nation. Most of these businesses report a rise in productivity, and a drop in absenteeism with relocation. Again, a positive change in conditions produces positive results.

In the past few years, the American shipping industry has been moving away from the practice of loading cargo with manpower and towards using the containers in which the cargo is shipped, stored and finally delivered by truck or train — without their being touched by human hands. Although dock workers are vehemently opposed to the idea, the new system is amazingly efficient. A cargo ship which once took 120 men a week to load can now be readied by about 60 men in a single day's time.

The Wall Street Journal, my favorite reading matter, ran an article recently about the Alcan Aluminum Plant in upstate New York. It seems the company has removed its time clock and break whistles. Workers now come and go as they choose. And if they grow tired of one function, they simply switch off with another employee. While it may sound chaotic, it really isn't. Tardiness and turnover have virtually disappeared. The plant boasts an absentee rate of 2.5%, as compared to the industry norm of 10%. And Alcan executives claim they can match the productivity of any factory in their industry.

If you've been paying attention, your cynicism should be gone by now. Creating positive conditions is a real and efficient tactic. And you can create the conditions that will promote efficiency and success in your office, too.

How important is environment to the average American? Look at the tremendous success of Muzak, that piped-in, commercial-free music you hear in restaurants, elevators, shopping centers, and during telephone calls while you're on "hold." When Muzak was first created, it was intended as a source of easy listening music, designed to create a comfortable atmosphere, conducive to just about anything. But the business boom Muzak produced came as a surprise to everyone, and brought money to the Muzak company. Studies showed that in grocery stores equipped with Muzak, shoppers tended to browse and buy for an average of two minutes longer than they did in a store without Muzak. And when inflation hit, and every company in America began trimming fat, Muzak suffered barely a scratch.

Make no mistake: conditions do not simply affect us. They control us in more ways than we realize. The right conditions produce success. The wrong conditions make even the best worker inefficient and unproductive.

How can you create the conditions that will bring higher profits, greater productivity, more satisfaction and less wasted time to your workplace or home? I have some ideas you may want to put into practice. I've organized these efficiency tips into several categories: habits, comforts, communication, structure, health, and motivation.

HABITS

So many of the things we do — and the things we don't do — are a result of repeated behavior that begins in youth and carries through the rest of our lives. Some habits are beneficial. Others are terribly destructive.

Some people feel they have no control over their habits. I disagree. Take smoking, for example. Lots of people say it's a habit they simply can't break. Why, then, have so many thousands of adult Americans managed to stop puffing and coughing in the past decade? It can be done. The secret lies in putting mind over body. It's the same kind of situation we talked about earlier in the chapters on goals and priorities. Even though you know how important it is for you to take action, you just never seem to get around to it.

The following three questions are designed to help you uncover your bad work habits, break them, and replace them with successful, money-making habits.

Question 1: What are your bad habits?

For the next few days, keep your eyes open for those repeated activities that waste time or produce bad work. Just about any non-productive activity could come under this heading: the long break you take each day, the two drinks you have at lunch, the clutter that builds up on your desk or in the kitchen sink. Try your best to identify the habits that are wasting your time, and you're one step closer to breaking them.

Question 2: Why do you do it?

The answer should be obvious. Look for the reasons like laziness, convenience, or long-established tradition. And keep in mind that just because you've always done something in a certain fashion doesn't mean you're doing it right.

Question 3: Why do you want to change?

Another easy question. You want to save time. You want to make more money. You want to move on to more important activities.

From now on, at the start of each day, ask yourself these three questions again. Make these three questions your first good habit. Remind yourself of what activity is hurting your business, why you continue to do it, and why you'd like to change. If you do this often enough, it's a lot like self-hypnosis. Within a short while, you should be sufficiently motivated to change.

Once you know what the problem is, it's time to form new, productive habits. And three similar questions are the key:

Question 1: What good work habits do you want to develop?

This could be anything from getting in to work a little earlier to cutting down your lunch hour or saving time at the supermarket. Whatever the preferred activity, it should placed at the dead center of your consciousness.

Question 2: Why do you want to do it?

Because it will lead to higher earnings, greater productivity and efficiency, or even more leisure time.

Question 3: Why do you want to change?

Because you're tired of wasting your life on useless, destructive activities.

Repeating these three good-habit questions every day could convince you that it's time to take bold action. Right now — today — you can begin to break the bad habits that hold you back, and form the good habits that will lead to success.

Every condition-creating tip in this chapter can be viewed as a good work habit. In fact, the entire Hour Power program comes under that same heading. If you find it difficult to perform any of the exercises or recommendations in this book, use these three good-habit questions to get yourself going. In time, efficiency will be your strongest tradition.

COMFORTS

At times it seems like the majority of America's work force is dissatisfied and frustrated. The lack of challenge, interest, and accomplishment seems to be at an all-time high among workers. But studies show that long before an employee begins to complain about these cerebral maladies, he is concerned and upset about a much more physical problem: the absence of simple creature comforts.

If you're trying to inspire your staff, or even just to motivate yourself, start with the basics. Hygiene comes first — your lavatory should be clean and comfortable. Next come food and drink. Be sure you have a working coffee machine. Order rolls or Danish every morning. Or get a small refrigerator where you can keep snacks, lunches, or beverages.

It's amazing how little things like this, when not supplied, make a worker feel unappreciated and ignored. Even a broken water cooler can destroy your desire to work hard.

Providing these basic comforts will cost a little money. But the improvement in your work will pay for them almost instantly.

COMMUNICATION

Perhaps more than any other single factor, a non-communicative atmosphere can make any operation unprofitable. When your employees or co-workers feel they cannot speak openly and honestly with you, they will have little desire to work hard or assist you in any way. And the same is true of repairmen, merchants, and salesmen.

One great way to save time is to spend time talking with the people at work. You should dedicate yourself to knowing as much as possible about your employees. Listen to their problems. Try to understand how they feel about you, their work, and their lives. Before you chastise someone for a job poorly done, ask them why they chose to handle matters as they did.

If an employee feels he can talk to you, that you are his

friend as well as his boss, he will be inspired to do his job well. His productivity will definitely increase.

Without doubt, communication is one of the strongest good-work conditions you can find. The time spent talking is never wasted. It is invested.

STRUCTURE

When evaluating the structure of your work place, be it office, factory or shop, there is one word that should be foremost in your mind: AVAILABILITY. By simply placing the tools or sources you need within easy reach, you can save several valuable hours every week.

For example, when the phone rings, what motion do you make to reach for it? Do you have to get up from your seat? Do you have to turn around? Do you have to take your eyes off the project you're working on?

Even if you only turn slightly to grab that ringing phone, you are wasting time. Chances are the call is a meaningless interruption, and you will momentarily return to your work. But now you must turn back, readjust your vision, and find your place. You've just wasted time. It doesn't seem like much, but over one year it will add up to several hours of your life that will never occur again.

Every item in your workplace should be positioned where you can reach out and grab it. For example, if you use reference books every day, place your desk next to the bookshelf. And why is your filing cabinet out in the hallway, where anyone who needs to delve into it must first walk to it? Every one of these steps is a waste of time. If you are trying to clean the bedroom, why is your broom in the basement?

If you have to talk to your secretary every ten minutes, why is her desk 20 feet away from yours? These little trips might be good for the leg muscles, but they don't increase productivity in the least.

Availability of information is vital to your associates and employees. Be sure any records, files, or reports they may need are out in the open, easily accessible to them. This will encourage them to take the incentive and allow them to avoid interrupting you.

Several other factors that relate to the structure of your work-place may also discourage good work. Studies have shown, for instance, that the higher the temperature in an office, or home, the lower the productivity. Keep your workplace at a nice, cool temperature. Not cold, of course, but not warm either. The cooler air is refreshing and inspires alert and clear thinking.

Noise is another destructive factor found in many work environments. To whatever degree possible, eliminate unnecessary noise at once. Extraneous sounds are disturbing, aggravating and distracting. Encourage your employees, and yourself, to concentrate by keeping things quiet. Radios and T.V. sounds never encourage efficiency.

Invite your associates to participate in the design of the workplace. Let them suggest new colors and decorations. If employees feel they have had some input into the environment they work in, they are much more likely to enjoy working.

HEALTH

More than ever before, we are aware of the vital link between mind and body. We know that depression can cause illness, and that poor health means poor work.

Many large companies have begun to supply employees with exercise facilities. Some workers now jog or swim rather than eat lunch. And for these organizations, the results have been profitable, indeed.

Perhaps you cannot afford to set up such an elaborate system, but you can encourage your employees to be healthy and keep fit. And you can surely try exercising once in a while yourself.

Make fitness a common topic of conversation around your office. Discuss sports and other healthy activities often. And start looking through the paper and magazines for articles about nutrition. Cut them out and post them where all your co-workers will be sure to take note.

Of course, you can't force someone else to be healthy. But you can create conditions that will encourage them.

MOTIVATION

The steps we've discussed so far will help you motivate your employees and yourself to do better work. But there are also some techniques that will directly reward your people for good work, and inspire them to make efficiency a regular practice.

Bonuses

Perhaps the greatest single motivation since God told Noah to build the Ark is a bonus. If an employee knows he will get money if he does good work, he will do good work. It's that simple. Try to give out bonuses often, and at unexpected times. B.F. Skinner told us years ago about the value of unexpected reward. So don't just wait for Christmas to hand out bonus-pay. Give it without warning, and you'll discover your workers are putting out all year long, not just before December.

Free Time

Give each worker an extra day off for each major jump in productivity. It seems surprising, but today's worker may find free time a bigger motivation than cash. And again, don't announce dates and deadlines for rewards. Give them out randomly, and at unexpected intervals. When a worker doesn't know when a reward will come, he is far more likely to work for it every day. If you're a housekeeper, be sure to give yourself free time as a reward or incentive.

Training

Unbelievable as it may seem, most businesses spend very little time training and educating the workers who spend their lives in service to the organization. The result is that a trainee may waste a year or more learning on his own what could have been taught in a few short weeks. Time spent on training is not wasted time. Again, it is an investment in the future.

Respect

Without question, a worker will be more motivated to do well if he or she feels respected. This has a lot to do with the communication problems we discussed earlier. Take the time to compliment people when they do things well. Show your high regard for them in front of clients and peers. Be certain good workers know you appreciate them.

Variety

If you deal with rather boring work, whether at home or on the job, a little variety can create miracles. This is the kind of situation where shifting priorities is a bonus. There is no greater source of unproductive, unhappy workers than the assembly-line. A toaster comes down the belt. You screw in two screws and put it back. Another toaster comes down the belt . . . and in half an hour, the worker is mentally in dreamland, screwing his screw in half-way, and letting every fourth toaster slip by. Break the monotony whenever you can. Have workers trade off jobs every few hours. Or let them stop one project and begin another. You will waste a little time. But if you dramatically boost productivity, you'll come out a winner.

By putting these principles to work for you, you will begin to create the conditions that lead to success. Some effort is involved, but the dividends are wonderful.

The next four chapters of this book concern the concepts that are the cornerstone of my Hour Power program. I call them "The Four D's."

Every time a new job comes onto your desk, you have four options: you can *drop it* — not accept the project at all; *delay it* — put it off for a later time; *delegate it* — give it to a subordinate to handle; or *do it* — get it out of the way right now, on your own.

Drop, Delay, Delegate or Do. The Four D's.

You already do these four things every day. The problem is that you do them incorrectly. If you know which of the Four D's is right for which job, and you can drop, delay, delegate, and do with efficiency and style, you can save tremendous amounts of time, make more money, and have more free time as well.

But the Four D's won't help you very much until you first create the conditions in which good work gets done. Take each of the good-work tips described in this chapter to heart, and you will soon see a turn-around in your working life.

5

Drop It

So clear I see, now it is done,
How I have wasted half my day,
And left my work just begun.

— Helen Hunt Jackson

Far too many years ago, when I was a young boy, my father told me a story about work — especially about working hard to meet the expectations of others. The story goes like this:

A farmer and his son, having had a particularly poor harvest and being in need of money, were taking one of their older mules into town to the monthly auction. It was a long journey from their remote farm into the village, so the boy and his father decided to ride the old mule.

During their trip, the travelers passed many other farmers and wanderers. And each person they passed had an opinion to express about this mule and its two masters.

The first person they passed took one look at the old mule and two riders and accused the farmer and his son of cruelty. "How can you treat a poor old mule like that?" the passerby exclaimed. Feeling guilty, the man and his son decided to take turns riding the mule.

First, the father rode the mule for a while. But soon, another passerby appeared and said, "What kind of father are you, riding comfortably on the mule while your son has to walk alongside?'' This made the father feel even more guilty than before, so he got down from the mule and let his son ride instead.

Then another passerby came along. "What kind of son are you?" he exclaimed. "A young boy riding on a mule while his poor old dad has to walk behind. Shame on you!" Now the boy was humiliated, and decided he preferred walking to experiencing this kind of social abuse.

Soon, the father and son were switching positions every few hundred yards. Up and down. Up and down. Finally, the father grew tired of all the climbing.

"Listen, son," the farmer told his boy. "What the hell. Let's carry the damn mule."

While the father got some rope out of his sack, the boy chopped a strong branch from a nearby tree. They bound the mule's legs, back and front, put the branch through the knots in the rope, and began carrying the mule.

The mule hung upside down, swaying gently in the breeze, while the farmer and his son struggled to hold him above ground. It was exhausting work, but they preferred it to the criticism they'd been getting before.

Soon, they drew near the village where this poor old mule would be sold. But first, they had to cross a river and climb up the other side.

Their attempt to cross that river was not very successful. The branch broke, the mule drowned, and the farmer and his son despondently headed back to the farm.

The moral of this story? If you try to please too many people, you wind up losing your ass.

I'd like to suggest that you — this very day — are working for too many people. You're doing too many things and trying to be everything to everyone. It isn't working — but you've spent so long doing it you now find it hard to stop.

You probably worked your way up from the bottom to the

top, making allies, impressing people, getting things done. No one helped you. No one handed it to you on a silver platter. You worked hard for what you have today.

And when things get rough, or a difficult project comes along, you still give it personal attention. When you want it done right, you do it yourself. And whatever comes into your office . . . whatever chore exists at home . . . you feel you have to handle it personally.

The end result? You're wasting your time. And not producing the kind of profits you should. I have an idea for you.

It's the first of the Four D's: Drop it.

Trying to do everything . . . trying to please everyone . . . this is the surest way to get nothing done. If you want to increase your own productivity and efficiency, the very first step is to learn to say no.

Have you ever noticed that people on the top executive level always feel free to say no? Learning to say no is one of the most difficult executive skills to acquire. It takes time, experience, and a certain amount of courageous self-assurance.

Most of us are downright fear-crazed. The idea of saying no absolutely terrifies us. We fear we will make enemies, alienate people, or destroy the alliances we have worked so hard to establish. Saying no is an action we never even contemplate seriously.

Well, I have some surprising information: saying no is often the best move you can make. It will make you a better businessman. It will, in time, produce in others a level of respect for you that may seem hard to believe. It will change your life.

Stop a minute and think about what you've done over the last five work days. Take a piece of paper and list the projects you've been working on. The first that come to mind are probably the high-priority jobs: an important account, a problem at home, a special deal the boss has asked you to handle.

But keep thinking a moment. Try to remember the little projects that you've spent some time on lately. A special favor for a friend. Double-checking on someone's work because they wanted your advice. It may even be something as important as opening junk mail that came into your office. How many low-priority activities like this have you handled in the past five days?

Now, stop thinking of those little activities as favors and obligations. Start thinking of them as wasted time. Consider how you might have used your time if those little, low-priority jobs had never turned up. Could you have done the big projects faster? Better? Could you have put the extra time to use pursuing one of your other goals?

If you can learn to drop just one minor activity today, you will become a better worker instantly. Even if it is just skipping one low-priority luncheon, you'll have more time to pursue the things that will bring you success. For every extra minute you can save is extra money you could be making, extra chores you could do.

Let's project ahead for a moment. Imagine that within a few weeks, you have begun to drop one minor activity every work day. Let's say the dropped item took an average of one half hour of your time each day. In just one week, you've saved two-and-a-half hours. That's over ten hours each month. And over 120 hours in a single year. By simply dropping a half hour of useless activity today, you are creating three full work weeks in your year. Now imagine dropping two half-hour activities every day . . . or three . . . or four . . .

But what items can be dropped so easily? How do you decide what's important and what isn't? How can you be sure a minor item, one that seems so profitless and wasteful, is not truly a gold mine in disguise?

Dropping — saying no — is an acquired skill. You will learn

it with time. Experience is unmistakably the best teacher when it comes to dropping.

A few months ago, I received a letter from someone who had attended one of my Hour Power seminars last year. It seems this man, a management consultant, had been particularly impressed with my speech . . . especially the section on dropping. He said it took him a little while to get up the nerve, but that finally he had learned how to say no.

A few weeks after hearing my lecture, this consultant received a phone call from a client he had worked with before. The client described a major project his organization was about to undertake. He expressed his interest in having the consultant's firm work with his organization. During his conversation, large sums of money were mentioned. To the naked eye, it looked like a great business opportunity.

But our friend was suspicious. It seems that in previous dealings with this client, he had run into some problems. At least twice before, this client had come to him with smaller projects. The consultant had agreed to a few preliminary meetings. Although these discussions provided the client with lots of information and advice, the deals had never gone through. The client had simply picked the consultant's brain and then said goodbye, I'll be in touch with you soon.

The consultant, after evaluating his experience with this client, decided to be bold and say no. He dropped the project. In fact, he refused to even discuss it.

The client was shocked. He soon telephoned one of our consultant's superiors and described his impertinent refusal to handle the project. The superiors were shocked. They pounced on our consultant and demanded an explanation.

The consultant told them about his past experiences with this client. And yet, the superiors were unconvinced. They decided to accept the client's offer and gave the account to another consultant in the firm. For several weeks, our bold dropper was in the dog house.

The second consultant, along with his assistant and his secretary, spent several weeks on the client's project. When he was finished, he presented his work to his superiors, who were quite pleased with him . . . and even more displeased with our dropping consultant.

Six months later, the client has yet to pay his bill to the firm. Our consultant friend is now a vice president. He has an office right next to those superiors who once admonished him. And he now says no quite frequently.

Learn it today: you can't please everyone. You can't do everything. You can't be everyone to everybody. It simply never works.

But where to stop doing everything and start dropping? Consider this example. I think it works as a guiding symbol for the entire concept of dropping.

Where is your "in" box? Probably on your desk, right above your "out" box. You take things out of the "in" box, work on them, and put them into the "out" box. The only thing that happens between "in" and "out" is your work. Try this idea. Put your "in" box on one side of your desk, and your "out" box on the other. And place your wastepaper basket next to the "in" box. As often as possible, drop something into the garbage. If, when you look in your "in" box, you should find a piece of mail offering a magazine or some other unimportant item, don't even open the envelope. Drop it in the garbage.

Suppose you find a letter from another department about some item that really doesn't concern you. Don't read it. Drop it in the garbage. Do the same thing with the junk mail you get at home.

How much time have you just saved? How much money? You saved five minutes reading the magazine promotion, and perhaps $20, had you taken the offer. You saved ten minutes by not reading the interdepartmental mail that didn't concern your office. In a few short moments you saved 15 minutes and $20.

Right now, you're probably feeling very hesitant about this whole idea of saying no. Don't worry, the feeling is completely natural. It took a long time for you to become as fear-crazed as you are. You can't expect to break the habit in a few minutes of reading.

The fear is natural. You're afraid of making mistakes. Afraid of dropping something important. You feel a tremendous need to cover for yourself. If you're like most people, you cover yourself so much that there's no time left to get anything important done.

You can't do both. You can't do everything. You must choose things to do, set priorities, and have the nerve to follow your own best judgment.

But how do you judge? What are the guidelines for dropping? The secret is forming objectives. You simply create certain criteria for what is worth your time and what isn't. You set up limits and boundaries on your activities. If a certain project does not fall within those boundaries, you say no and drop it.

At times, dropping seems like a frivolous decision. You may feel a little like you're cutting off your right arm. But if your objectives are correct, you will eventually come out ahead.

Here's another story from *The Wall Street Journal* that will help illustrate my message:

In the summer of 1978, the Lewis and Clark Mercantile Bank, situated in St. Louis, lost some 3,600 checking accounts. Since they only had a total of about 16,000 accounts, this was a loss of more than 20 percent of their customers. The amazing thing is that they lost these customers intentionally. The bank dropped them.

It seems the bank decided to charge checking account holders $3 each month for this service that had formerly been free. When the new charge was announced, 3,600 check writers decided to take their money elsewhere.

What happened to the bank's economic picture? It brightened considerably. They tripled their earnings. They cut payroll and paperwork. And they freed bank personnel to work on important matters.

There is the number one reason for dropping: profit. If you analyze your operation you will find many areas where less work and fewer clients can mean more profits.

The secret is forming objectives, having hard facts and reliable information from which you can make tough decisions and take aggressive action. If you set your objectives correctly, you will see what must be dropped, you will learn when to say no.

Here's another example of dropping, this one from *Time* magazine:

Pacific Southwest Airlines, a rapidly growing concern, has decided that some of its past activities were overly ambitious. It seems they had bought into several industries besides air transport: radio stations, car rentals, and hotels. Although these interests began with losses, PSA's management hoped that, in time, they could become profitable.

But PSA's primary operation — the airline itself — is developing so quickly that management has decided they cannot waste time on outside concerns. They have dropped the other businesses, and put their full attention into transportation.

The second great reason for dropping: saving time. With objective priorities, you can see what projects are truly important and which simply keep you from tackling your high-priority business.

In general, it can be stated that any activity that is not profitable, or which keeps you from more worthwhile things, should be dropped. When you find one of these items on your desk, say no. When a chore or errand like this comes up at home, say no.

The way to uncover and expose drop items is evaluation. Every time you begin a new task, and every time you look in your "in" box, you must evaluate the priorities at hand. Think of your objectives, and decide how this project fits in. Remember your boundaries, and then see where this new piece of work falls. If the activity is unprofitable, wasteful or distracting from more important work, drop it at once.

Besides this moment to moment evaluation, yearly investigations of your entire operation are absolutely essential. The system you should be using is "Zero Based Budgeting."

A term popularized by the Carter Administration, Zero Based Budgeting is actually a simple concept. It means you go back to the very beginning and evaluate every single aspect of your operation, from your filing system, through your letterhead, and all the way up to your biggest and most profitable activities. With Zero Based Budgeting, nothing is sacred. Nothing is left unchanged because of tradition, or because you've always done things this way, or for any other reason except profit. If it works, keep it. If it doesn't, drop it.

Let's say in your annual evaluation you discover that the system of paper shuffling you've used since your first job is outdated. The rest of your company is using a new system that eliminates one copy of every single piece of paper work. But you're so accustomed to your system, you've grown so comfortable with it, it works for you and you'd like to keep it.

Nothing is sacred. Drop your system and accept the new one. Your objective is profit and time saving. The old system doesn't fall inside those boundaries. It's time to say no to yourself.

How many such activities are you presently canonizing without realizing it? The answer lies with you. Every office will have a different set of circumstances, different priorities and unique problems. But here's a list of 20 time-wasting activities you may want to drop.

1.	Bad Clients:	Never do anything for a client who didn't come through in the past. You're just repeating mistakes.
2.	Deadbeats:	Don't perform services for people who take forever to pay their bills.
3.	Cheap Work:	If you've got anything better to do, don't work for less than your standard fee. Set objectives and stick with them.
4.	Re-Do's:	Nine times out of ten, reworking a project is a waste of time and brings no profit.
5.	Repeats:	Repeating a single function over and over again is like paying a bill twice: you lose money on the deal.
6.	Double-Ups:	Don't spend time on any project someone else is also working on.
7.	Waste Paper:	Why do you need three copies of meaningless notes? Cut paperwork and save time.
8.	Busy Work:	Those things you do when you can't think of anything else to do. Set priorities and you'll never be idle again.
9.	Distractions:	Don't miss important opportunities because you're busy doing low-priority work. Anything that keeps you from profitable activities should be dropped.
10.	Fun:	Work you enjoy may not be work you profit from. Remember your objectives, and drop anything that isn't bringing you nearer to your goals.
11.	Friends:	Don't give free work to people because you like them. Be diplomatic and tell your friends you're busy trying to succeed.

12.	Bonuses:	Unless a client is constantly working with you, don't give him free time. When the job is done, move on to new business. Let the client pay you if he wants your services.
13.	Fear Work:	Pointless activities you undertake to protect yourself from unidentified assailants. Do the job right and you won't have to cover for anybody.
14.	Socializing:	How many times do you call clients and associates just to stay friendly? Cut the number in half and save a few days every year.
15.	Mail:	Up to half of the mail you receive can probably be dropped. Better still, have your secretary drop it for you.
16.	Speculation:	Unless you have lots of free time (and you don't), stop working on projects before you agree on fees. No pay, no work.
17.	Mistakes:	Don't follow through on projects you accepted and now want to reject. Go ahead and back out of the deal. There are more important matters to concern yourself with.
18.	Favors:	Never do work for friends in other departments. If an activity is not your responsibility, drop it at once.
19.	Systems:	If your system or style of doing any activity is outdated, drop it and learn the new way.
20.	Technology:	Any outdated machinery or technology, whether it's your typewriter or your stove, is holding you back. Invest in the new equipment and stay up-to-date on technology improvements.

Your wasteful activities may be a little different, or may be much more numerous. But if you set firm objectives and use

Zero Based Budgeting to evaluate your performance, you can isolate the droppable items and get rid of them today.

Of course, the tendency to fear is powerful, and you'll have some trouble when you first begin to say no. One way to make it easier is to psych yourself up for it, just like an athlete psychs himself for a big game.

Think of all the reasons why you don't want to do a particular job. It won't make any money for you. It will keep you from getting more important things done. You just don't feel like it. Let your natural laziness work for you. Tell yourself over and over again that this project is a complete waste of your time and an insult to your intelligence. Then, when you're angry enough, turn around and say no.

The best medium for saying no is the printed word. Write a brief letter, stating simply that you have decided not to undertake a particular project. Keep your words simple and direct. Don't try to argue your point, don't give reasons for your decision. Just announce your firm commitment to say no.

If necessary, circulate the letter. Get as many names involved as possible. Show it to all the possible committees who might have some input on the topic. Then wait awhile to be sure there are no objections, and send the rejection letter off to the client or whoever is concerned.

You've done it! You've said no! Now you can get back to the high-priority projects that can help you be successful.

When in doubt about dropping, ask yourself these vital questions:

What Are My Objectives? Have an exact picture of your needs and requirements. Use hard facts and numbers to evaluate your own most important goals.

What Priority is This Activity? Use your objectives to determine how essential any activity is to your business. Give the activity in question a rank: high, medium, low, or none.

How Does it Compare with Other Work? Establish priority

levels of the projects you're currently working on. Decide where this new activity fits in.

Will This Keep Me from High Priority Business? Be certain the new project will not interfere with activities of greater importance to you.

If, after asking these questions, you find yourself facing a low or zero priority task that does not meet your objectives and interferes with higher priority work, you are on the brink of dropping. But one last question remains to be answered.

Do I Have to Do This? If a superior has voiced particular interest in a certain activity, or if legal requirements are forcing your hand, you cannot drop the activity.

But if you don't have to do something useless, drop it. Say no. And save yourself time for valuable things.

6

Delay It

Let all things be done decently and in order.

— Corinthians, I, 14

How many mornings are you late for work in an average month? Two? Three? More? What do you do first when you get to the office or begin housework? If you're like most people, you start with a few easy tasks and gradually get adjusted to being in your office. You save the harder work for later on, maybe after lunch, when you'll be more alert and ready to dedicate yourself.

Which day of the week is your least productive? Chances are, Monday is your "off" day. Monday seems to be an off day for everyone. Some people spend the entire day getting over the weekend and returning to the flow of business life. In terms of productivity, Monday is a complete waste.

Think back to the last time you overslept. What happened that morning? Chances are once you finally got out of bed, everything went exactly as not planned. Your train was delayed. You lost your briefcase. Amazingly, everyone else was on time that morning. Even the weekly meeting scheduled for 10.30 started on time.

This probably sounds all too familiar to you. If so, you are doing things backwards. Instead of getting your hardest work out of the way first thing in the morning, you put it off for

73

afternoon. Instead of getting a jump on your week by using Monday wisely, you waste it completely. Instead of getting an early start on your life, you spend a few extra minutes in bed.

Now stop and think back to your goals in life. These are the things you work for, the matters most important to you, the areas of life you want most to have go well. Would you avoid the fulfillment of these goals? If you could have exactly what you want, whenever you want it, would you delay, avoid, or procrastinate?

Of course not. But that is exactly what you are doing. When you delay work, you delay success. If you want the wealth and respect that comes from achievement, why do you hate going to work?

There are two kinds of delay: positive and negative. Positive delay helps you get things done faster and better. Negative delay ruins your life.

Let's talk about negative delay first. A more common name for it is procrastination. There are many ways to procrastinate. You probably practice a few of them every day. Saying "I'll get to it in a minute," or intentionally misplacing something important. Whatever method you use, it's easy to find a way to procrastinate.

The problem is that you may be delaying bigh priority work that will bring you closer to your life's goal, yet you are trying to side-step it.

Why do we procrastinate? There are seven basic reasons:

1. It seems too time consuming. Without any logical reason, you decide an important job will take too much time. So you opt to let it go for later and work now on less important, less profitable work. Laziness and waste.

2. It's a long range project. Lots of important activities are spread over long periods of time. But like a kid in school, you let it go to the last minute. Then you do a poor job and wind up with nothing.

3. Non-immediate importance to you. Even though you may know a certain project is high priority, it just doesn't strike you as important this morning. So you let it go for later.

4. You haven't made a commitment. It's an important job, but you haven't promised to do it yet. And you haven't committed yourself to getting it done right. Why not procrastinate and relax?

5. Doing it now will be unpleasant. The work is difficult, or will interfere with something you enjoy doing. No matter how much goal-success it may bring, you just don't feel like it.

6. You don't have a deadline. No one has told you exactly when this job needs to be done, so you simply let it sit.

7. You see no immediate profit. Even though your objectives describe this job as high priority, you have yet to see any instant profit from it, so you delay it.

These are all the wrong reasons for delaying. If you delay something for these reasons, you are wasting time. This kind of delay is very definitely negative.

There is only one good reason to delay. A project should be delayed if it holds you back from a higher priority activity, but cannot be dropped. Putting off one job until a more important one is completed is positive delay.

You probably create negative delays every working day. When you do easy work in the morning and save the harder work for later, you are procrastinating. When you decide to waste Monday, you are procrastinating. You can always find a good reason to procrastinate, or at least a good excuse.

Just think a moment about your policy of saving harder work for the afternoon. I call it the Tomorrow System.

First thing in the morning, you schedule your day. You decide to leave Project A, your highest priority, for this afternoon. You spend the morning on other activities.

This afternoon, you try to get started on Project A. You muddle around with it, wondering how you can get away without doing it. A few phone calls interrupt you. Co-workers come into your office for information. By five o'clock, you have done only a small amount of work on Project A.

Before you know it, tomorrow is here and Project A is still awaiting your undivided attention. But first, you decide to work on a few easier, lower priority items to get yourself going. Soon, it's afternoon again. More interruptions. More phone calls.

The next thing you know, it's Friday afternoon and Project A is still sitting, not done.

What are the effects of this kind of procrastination? Guilt and anxiety. Your conscience keeps saying, "do Project A!" And you keep avoiding, delaying, making excuses.

Soon you feel a lot of stress about Project A. It worries you so much you don't even want to think about it. And before you know it, you're creating extra work for yourself. You are writing memos and making up reasons why Project A isn't completed yet.

The final step in the procrastination process is one of the most unrecognized forms of negative delay: perfectionism. When you finally get around to attacking Project A, with a complete dedication to finish it right now, you are so concerned about it that you labor over it at great length. You question every decision you make. You go back and re-do the small amount of work you already did. And Project A winds up taking longer than it ever should have.

How do you beat this procrastination cycle? You return to your goals.

Go back to those four life goals you established earlier. Remind yourself of how important they are to you. Now take a look at your priority chart for today. The highest priority item is the one which will bring you closest to those goals you long to fulfill.

Now, create objectives. Your first objective should be to accomplish your high priority activities as soon as possible (that means right now). You should never put off high priority items for later in the day. Do them now, this very moment, if you truly intend to get them done at all.

Next, commit yourself to attaining your objectives. Decide now to get an early jump on your day. Set your alarm clock early, and you'll give yourself the extra time you'll need to handle problems and leap over hurdles.

Starting early is a vital concept in the Hour Power system. And it really isn't hard to do. Of course, if you work more efficiently later in the day, you still need to get started when you hit your peak. The principle's the same, no matter what time of day: get going! Just remind yourself that you want success, you want to achieve your goals.

Then accept the fact that if you want something you must work for it now. That means doing the hard work first. Getting up before you have to. And getting the week's hardest projects done on Monday.

Not procrastinating is a new way of life for you. And it's going to be a bit of a shock at first. Of course, the same can be said about the new success you will find once you stop wasting time.

But what about positive delay? When is delaying work the best thing you can do? How do you identify the activities which should be delayed?

Positive delaying is a lot like dropping: it lets you get on to more important matters. As a rule, you should drop everything you possibly can. If there is any way in this world to get the activity out of the way, drop it by all means.

But if you find yourself stuck with low priority items you simply can't drop, delay them for later. Put your mind on high priority business for now, and do the less important activities when you're finished.

What items should be delayed? There are three categories:

1. *Emotional Activities.* One of the most time wasting projects you'll ever handle are the ones you get emotional about. And this can mean any kind of emotion. Maybe it's a certain account that causes anger. Something you feel has been screwed up and passed along by goldbricks until it finally wound up on your desk. Delay a project like this as long as possible. Let it sit, and try not to think about it. The last thing you want to do is run around criticizing and shouting out of pure anger or frustration. The longer you delay this activity, the more calm and reasonable your treatment of it will be.

   Another emotional project might be something you're doing out of friendship or from obligation. If you can't drop a project like this, the very least you can do is delay it.

   Watch out also for activities that excite or challenge you. Excitement and challenge are great emotions, but they can be misdirected or unfounded. Again, delay this kind of project and see how excited you are about it later.

2. *Low Priority Activities.* Every day, you should be reviewing your goals and determining priorities. Remind yourself of your objectives and decide how important a particular project really is. If it's top priority, do it right away. If it has a medium or low priority, delay it until the more essential work is done.

3. *Projects with Incomplete Information.* All too often, you find a job awaiting your attention that you'd like to accomplish, but can't because you lack certain vital information. The project may even be top priority, but still you lack the facts you need to do it right. Rather than trying to accomplish this project without the tools you need, set it aside for later. This way, you can wait for the information and

do the job in one sitting, instead of breaking it up, spreading it out, and shifting activities. In the meantime, let your assistants or secretary get the information you need.

When you come across projects that fit into any of these three categories, delay them promptly. You will now be free to do the work that needs doing most.

You probably do a lot of positive delaying every day. The problem is you don't have this system working for you. You can't objectively state why you're delaying. And you're not delaying correctly.

Most people, when deciding to let one activity go for a while and complete another first, make the mistake of leaving the delayed project sitting right in front of them on the desk. Usually, they do this so they won't accidentally forget the delayed item.

But what happens? While doing the high priority work, these people find themselves glancing over at the delayed project. They lose concentration for a second and think, "I've got this other job to do today. Can't forget about it." Now they turn back and try to remember where they were on the first project. The result? Wasted time. A self-induced interruption. More guilt and anxiety.

When you go through your "in" box each morning, take the items you've decided to delay and place them on a table next to your desk. Do not place them on the desk itself. This way, you will have a neat, organized stack of delayed work, right where you can find it, but also where it won't interrupt you.

I recently made a little study among some of the executives and homemakers who attend my seminars. I asked them to categorize by project the phone calls they receive each day. Excluding personal calls, the interruptions broke down like this:

Work doing right now	— 10%
Work in the future	— 17%
Work delayed	— 70%
Unclear	— 3%

Seventy percent of all incoming calls concerned work the executives were delaying. This shouldn't really come as a surprise. Most of your phone calls probably ask, "Are you doing this yet?" or "When are you going to get to this?" When you delay work, it benefits you, but may greatly excite others.

Based on this fact, where would the best place be to put your phone? Next to your delay pile. This way, you can get to it easily when the phone calls come in. You'll save a few moments of spinning, turning and searching for paper work.

Perhaps you think I'm being a little compulsive about saving a few seconds here, a half minute there. If you feel that way, it's simply because you don't understand yet.

If you can begin today to stop wasting those unnoticed seconds and half-minutes, you will soon find you have more time, more chances to make money, more leisure. Believe it or not, when you save a few seconds, you are effectively increasing your life span.

Another useful tip for positive delaying is to always let your co-workers, assistants, secretary, or family members, know exactly what projects you've put on hold. If they are aware of what you're doing — and not doing — they can help you do it right. Your secretary can fend off interrupting clients on the telephone who are panicking about projects you've delayed. And your assistants can be preparing the delayed project for your attention.

There is still one form of procrastination we haven't discussed. It's called muddling. Although you haven't delayed a project — you're working on it right now — you are dragging your feet. Chances are you're motivated by a negative delay reason. You don't feel like doing this . . . it's unpleasant . . . you don't see any immediate reward . . . and so on. Even though you resolved yourself to do this project, you are doing it so slowly and poorly that your work is wasted. Muddling is one of the top time wasters I know of.

When you decide to do something, decide also to do it right. We'll talk more about doing things right later on.

When you start making an effort to stop procrastinating you should be prepared for a shock. You will find so many places in your life where you procrastinate and delay without good reason that it may be overwhelming. And you may have a very hard time breaking these old bad habits.

Here's a tip: put that guilt and anxiety to work for you. Create a procrastination pile beside your desk. This is not for items you are delaying for good reasons. This pile should only contain the items you're avoiding out of laziness or lack of motivation.

Let the procrastination sit there and grow. Take a look at it when you have a free moment. The guilt should be growing as steadily as the procrastination pile itself.

Soon, the pile will be too large and you'll need a procrastination drawer. Select a drawer you'll find hard to overlook. Open the drawer a few times every day and let yourself have an anxiety attack.

Now, stop and think about your goals. Remember what you said about success? Money? Personal Growth? Taking care of your family? Look at your procrastination file. Is this your idea of working for your goals? Is procrastination the road to success and happiness? Why are you doing this to yourself? To your family?

The guilt should be overwhelming. If this doesn't motivate you to stop procrastinating, you may well be a lost cause.

Delaying work is one of the great American pastimes. Unfortunately, few of us do it right.

I'm reminded of an article I read about a rather unusual group of people: the Procrastinator's Club of America. This is an organization of people who are dedicated to putting things off forever. The president of the club once quoted his membership at almost 500,000, but added that "most of our members haven't gotten around to joining yet."

Finally, let me point out one of the great distinctions between negative and positive delays. When you delay important work for the wrong reasons, you eventually wind up in trouble. But when you delay for the right reasons, activities sometimes have a way of becoming zero priority. At this point, you can drop them.

Imagine if you had that kind of luck just once a week? How much time could you save? A few hours now? A few days this year? A few months of your life?

Like everything else, there is a right way and wrong way to delay. If you learn how to do it right, you can save time, and get important things done faster and better. Don't look now, but that's the real road to success.

7

Delegate It

The best executive is the one who has sense enough to pick good men to do what he wants done and the self-restraint to keep from meddling with them while they do it.

— Theodore Roosevelt

At some point before the dawn of civilization, two cavemen found themselves in need of something to eat. As luck would have it, one of the cavemen had recently discovered that if you take a big stick and hit an animal over the head with it, dinner was served. After this brilliant realization, the fellow took to calling himself "the boss." In exchange for food, the second caveman, who had recently been named "flunky," would happily perform the menial tasks of cave life: cleaning out the den, watching for attackers, and carrying out the garbage.

As the boss and the flunky wandered about the steamy countryside, searching for something to eat, they came upon a saber-toothed tiger. Having never dealt with so ferocious an animal before, the boss decided to enlist the flunky's help.

They followed the saber-toothed tiger until he wandered into a nearby cave. While the animal rested inside, the boss quietly explained his attack plan to the flunky.

"You take the stick," the boss whispered, "and climb up on

top of the cave entrance. Then I'll run around out front until the tiger comes out to get me. Then, when he comes through the entrance, you smash him.''

"Wordlessly, the flunky took the stick and tiptoed up to the ledge right over the entrance to the cave. When he was well positioned, the boss began running around, flailing his arms, shouting caveman obscenities, and generally antagonizing the tiger into an attack.

Just as expected, the tiger came bounding out of his cave, growling and drooling, ready to eat. At precisely the correct moment, the boss looked up at the flunky and shouted ''Now!''

The flunky looked back at the boss and replied, ''Now what?''

The tiger enjoyed his meal. The flunky sneaked away from the scene while the tiger was busy eating. The secret of successful hunting, having never been shared by the boss, was not re-discovered for several hundred years.

I hope this little story illustrates the origins of one of mankind's most enduring — and incorrect — natural tendencies: Do-it-yourselfism. "If you want a job done right, do it yourself," the old saying goes, and most of us believe it. But the fact of the matter is that doing it yourself is often impossible. The very nature of management — of executive functioning — is to delegate work to others. But it's important (as the "boss" discovered) to know how and what to delegate.

Advancing up the corporate ladder involves much more than increased earnings, promotions, a larger office, and a key to the executive washroom. The climb upward also includes a shift from doing everything on your own to having others begin to do things for you. Management is delegation, and delegation is the art of using your time to manage other people's time and work.

But somehow, the transition often does not occur as it should. Most people begin their careers at the bottom of their industry, or some place quite near the bottom. Here, they are trained to perform a specific task. And if they do that job well, they are soon promoted.

The next step will probably bring new responsibilities and tasks. The employee's outlook on his industry begins to broaden as he learns more and handles more intricate duties. Ironically, he may soon discover that he no longer performs the functions he mastered, did well, and earned promotion by doing.

The employee's ability to adapt to this change will make or break him in business. If he insists on continuing the old habits of do-it-yourselfism, he will wind up wasting a lot of time, his own, his superiors', and his employees'. If, on the other hand, he learns to successfully delegate the right work . . . to the right people . . . in the right way, he will continue to climb that corporate ladder until he reaches the top.

I call this change from doing everything to the effective use of delegation "The Vital Shift." It is this shift of activity that makes the progress of anyone in business from worker to executive, from labor to management.

As a businessman moves forward in his career, he begins to spend more time telling others what to do and less time doing it himself. By its very nature, executive responsibility defies the do-it-yourself principle. If he is to succeed, today's businessman must be expert at the art of delegation. He must know what jobs to delegate, who to give them to, and how to be certain the work will get done correctly, quickly and thoroughly. And a homemaker must delegate to the spouse, the children, and other helpers.

But being in the position to delegate does not necessarily produce the ability to delegate correctly. In fact, many top executives are actually very poor delegators. They assign projects without fully understanding the work. They give the job to the wrong person in their organization. The work gets done poorly, and after lots of wasted time, they wind up doing the job themselves anyway.

Delegation is one of the most delicate, and difficult, of skills. It requires awareness and sensitivity. It involves investigation, evaluation, and creative decision making.

Poor delegation can cause so many problems that not delegating at all would be a better alternative. Poor delegation destroys employee morale and wastes time and money. Those on the receiving end of poor delegation refer to is as "passing the buck" or "dumping."

Correct delegation, however, is the ultimate source of efficiency and productivity. It makes the most of your time, your employee's time, and your company's payroll dollars. When an executive can effectively delegate work to his employees, he can assure the proper completion of his duties, create inspired, satisfied subordinates, and develop a well-run organization.

In delegation, an executive assigns an activity, interaction, or object to an employee. The employee is given the authority to complete the assignment within a specified period of time. Accountability is created and assigned, as is incentive. Although responsibility for the project remains with the executive, the employee attains a sense of responsibility and accountability for the work, and he is therefore motivated to complete it efficiently.

Delegation takes time. The time is spent planning, communicating, supervising, motivating and even correcting. So much initial time is required for effective delegation that you may be tempted to avoid the entire process.

Do yourself a favor and reconsider. One-man bands survive only in circuses and carnivals, where they play for laughs. Great conductors lead major symphonies, earn high pay, and become famous. You can't be a success in the business world, or any other aspect of life, if you try to lead the band and play all the instruments at the same time.

You must accept the fact that you will spend working hours learning to delegate efficiently. And if the long-term benefits aren't enough to convince you, consider the fact that when you delegate work effectively you are saving money. When you save company money, everyone profits.

How much money can you save through delegation? Stop a moment and calculate your own cost-per-hour value. Now imagine how expensive your correspondence would be if you were typing your own letters instead of giving them to your secretary. You probably type at less than half her rate. You get paid at least double her salary. You make more typing errors. By delegating your typing to her, you are saving money and time.

Once you've established the practice of delegation, "managing by exception" will become the rule. Routine items will be taken care of automatically, without your involvement. Only exceptional problems with exceptional circumstances will be brought to you by your subordinates.

If you are not delegating the majority of your work right now, you must ask yourself why not. In most cases, a failure to delegate is caused by barriers inside yourself.

Some businessmen are afraid to delegate work because they assume others will say "He never does anything. His staff does all the work." But if the company expected you to do everything by yourself, why do you have assistants, secretaries, and subordinates?

Other executives fail to delegate because they fear their employees will take credit for the work. They refuse to admit that others have capabilities, or may even be more qualified than they for a specific activity. In reality, just the opposite is the case. If you've been in business for a while, you know that the boss always gets credit for everything. The common problem is that this boss does not pass that praise along to his subordinates, leaving them frustrated and unmotivated.

Still others fear that gifted employees will threaten their positions. They hesitate to reward and educate a talented young assistant because they feel uncertain of their own standing in the corporation. And some executives are just afraid of causing conflict. They feel that delegating work will anger or upset employees. I've met other businessmen who refuse to delegate because they distrust their employees, or believe that only they themselves can do the job right.

These fears and failures are motivated by insecurity, anxiety, and are completely unfounded. You must recognize these crippling doubts, overcome them, and boldly begin to delegate work, whether to employees at the office or to children and other family members at home.

The first prerequisite to effective delegation is knowledge. Knowledge of the nature of the project, its unique characteristics and problems, the abilities and desires of your staff, and the overall objectives of your department or company. This knowledge can be gained by following the seven-step "Effective Delegation System."

But before you begin the system, ask yourself these questions:

1. Can someone do this project instead of me?
2. Might someone else be able to do it better?
3. Could someone else accomplish it at less expense?
4. Can someone else do it with better timing?
5. Will delegating this project contribute to the training and development of my staff?

If you answered any of these questions affirmatively, it's time to start delegating.

Here are the seven steps to Effective Delegation:

1. Select the activity, interaction or objective to be delegated.
2. Choose the person to whom this work will be given.

3. Determine the time, situation and method of delegation.
4. Create an exact plan for delegation.
5. Delegate the work.
6. Monitor the employee's progress.
7. Review and evaluate your success.

If you follow these seven steps carefully and thoroughly, you will increase your knowledge of your operation, improve the efficiency of your department, free yourself for matters only you can handle, motivate your staff, give them additional training and knowledge, and create a delegation system which will work for you day in and day out.

Let's go through these seven steps one by one, seeing how each should be done and isolating common problems and mistakes.

STEP ONE: *Select the Activity to Be Delegated.*

As a general rule, you should delegate any project which someone else can handle. But in order to do this, you must first have an understanding of the activity and capabilities of those who work below you. The only way to achieve this understanding is through evaluation.

Examine the project under consideration carefully. Be sure you understand what needs to be done, what special aspects or intricacies this activity involves. If you are not fully aware of what the project involves and what results are desired, do not delegate it until you are.

When you understand the project, ask yourself how well you can make others understand it. Be sure you have some plan for explaining the nature and objective of the activity to the person who will handle it. Also, try to be certain that this work will give some new knowledge or experience to the employee.

Finally, ask yourself how much control you will have over

the project once it has been delegated. If there is no way to remain aware of the progress of the assignment after you've delegated it, you may wish to keep this job for your own attention.

Avoid delegating 'hot potatoes' — special projects that have a very high priority level and require your immediate attention. An example of a hot potato is a specific activity which your superiors have voiced a very strong interest in. This kind of job should be done by you. Also, never delegate any project which is confidential. If the activity involves special information that only you should be aware of, don't hand it out to others.

STEP TWO: *Choose the Person to Whom This Work Will be Given.*

It is recommended that you undertake a full evaluation of your staff. During the next few days, have every employee in your department create a written critique of his or her responsibilities and functions. Ask them to tell you honestly which projects they enjoy, which they consider below their position, and what new activities they think they could be handling. Then, have a staff meeting. Let each of your employees present his or her critique. Invite comment from other employees. Look in particular for areas where two employees' activities cross. If any members of your staff have strong objections or criticisms of others, give them some of your time for private discussion.

There are two factors that you should be looking for in staff evaluations: knowledge and completion speed. You must discover how much knowledge your staff has of their jobs.

You may discover that one or two employees are far more knowledgeable of your operation than you formerly believed them to be. These people may have unique talents and abilities that will make them perfect candidates for high-level delegation.

Completion speed is another vital factor. For example, you may learn that one secretary can type at twice the rate of another. Or that one assistant can accomplish difficult tasks in almost half the time it takes another to do similar work.

Once you have established the knowledge and completion speed of each worker, you can estimate which projects each person can handle. Now you can return to your analysis of the work you wish to delegate and determine which projects your staff can complete to the satisfaction of your objectives.

Your staff analysis, if successful, makes this step easy. Return to the two major criteria of that analysis: knowledge and completion speed. Then decide if you want the job done brilliantly or quickly. Naturally this objective will immediately show you the right person for the job. Of course, if you're lucky, your most knowledgeable employee will also be your most efficient. Avoid the tendency to give this person all your work.

But other considerations also come into play. Time value is one important factor. Don't assign low priority projects to employees who carry a high time value for your company. This kind of poor delegating will not only waste money, it will also demoralize and unmotivate your staff.

Also, keep in mind a principle I call the "Learning Curve." That is, the longer an employee is on your staff, the more knowledge he or she will attain. Thus, a newer employee will require more training and instruction, while a more experienced employee will be ready to handle most jobs on his own. This element of training is essential both to effective delegation and the improvement of your operation. It will take time at first, but as the learning curve progresses, so will you and your employees.

Consider training value when you delegate work. At times, it may be wise to give a medium-level priority to a new or less experienced employee. The project will excite, motivate and instruct him. But be careful not to burden employees with projects they really can't handle. This will only produce confused, pressured people who fear going to work in the morning.

Using knowledge, completion time, time value, and training value, you can select the right employee or family member for the right project.

STEP THREE: *Determine the Time, Situation, and Method of Delegation.*

Most executives delegate work at the worst possible time of day: first thing in the morning. While this might be convenient for you, it is a major disincentive for your staff. Consider how they feel: they've come to work with a rough idea of what they will be doing today, and suddenly this new project is thrown into their lap. Schedules must be changed, priorities shifted. Time is wasted from beginning to end.

The best time to delegate is the last thing in the afternoon. This allows your employees to prepare for tomorrow's work today, to ready themselves and prepare schedules. They will return to work the next day having slept on this new project, and ready to attack it. At home, delegate chores to family members after dinner or later in the evening.

Face to face delegation is the best kind. It allows you to answer questions, invite feedback, and use your facial expression and body language for emphasis. Only the most unimportant projects should be delegated via a memo. Remember: if you want your staff to feel motivated and excited by a project, they must believe it is important enough to deserve a little of your time. Writing memos may be fast and easy, but it does not give the impression of importance.

Some operations may present geographical barriers to face to face delegation. Sometimes, you are on a different floor of a building than your employees. Other executives find themselves dealing with branch managers or salesmen, at times having to delegate over a few hundred miles of telephone wire. If this is the case, the face to face method is out. The telephone is still preferable to a memo. It retains some element of personal involvement. If there is no alternative, send the employee a memo outlining the job and ask them to call you as soon as possible.

Delegation is a personal matter. It is you entrusting important work to someone below you. If possible, do it in person.

STEP FOUR: *Create an Exact Plan for Delegation.*

Before you delegate a project, you must have highly defined objectives. Who should handle this job? Why have you selected this person? How long should the project take? What results are desired? Where are the resources they may need? How can they inform you of their progress?

You must have a solid answer for each of these questions before the work is delegated. It may be wise to put these objectives in writing, give a copy to the employee and keep one for your records. This way, you are both fully aware of the boundaries and characteristics of the project and there should be no room left for misunderstanding.

This delegation plan will guide you through the rest of the effective delegation process.

STEP FIVE: *Delegate the Work.*

The way you handle delegation — the style you display, the words and phrases you use — will have a tremendous effect on the performance of your helpers. This communication process has three major objectives: to explain the project completely, to establish guidelines and criteria, and to motivate the worker.

Before you delegate the project, it is wise to tell the employee (or family member) why he or she has been chosen for this duty. The secret here is to accentuate the positive. Point out the particular skills or abilities that make this employee the right person for this job. Emphasize the trust and belief you have in this person. Be sure they know you consider them capable of the work. And also, make it clear that they are responsible for the successful completion of the activity involved. Make sure they know that this work will reflect on them and influence their standing with the organization, both now and in the future.

When explaining the nature and objectives of the task, tell the employee all you know. Don't set hidden traps they may fall into later by withholding information now. Give all the aims involved: who wants this done, who you are answerable to for this work, who the client is, etc. Tell them about your work in this area in the past. Let them know how things have been handled before, and what results were achieved.

Be sure the helper fully understands the result you expect. If possible, list hard facts, numbers and goals. In other words, "this should be taken care of soon" is not a sufficient explanation.

Give the employee a hard deadline to work toward. Let him know that only the worst of circumstances should push this project beyond its deadline. Tell him how this deadline was arrived at and why it seems fair to you. Also, set a schedule for progress reports. Tell the employee when he should get back to you with information about the job. And give him some idea what you will expect to see at each of these check points.

Finally, motivate the helper to perform well by giving him the freedom to perform the task in his own way. Creativity is an uncommon quality, and it should be developed whenever possible. If an occasional mistake is the cost of creativity, the long-range benefits will far outweigh the immediate risks.

Don't insist your employees handle this project exactly as it was handled last time. Show your trust in them by inviting them to develop new approaches and techniques to old jobs. Let them look for excess work, time wasters, double-ups. Let them create their own system for accomplishing the work within the guidelines you have set.

But don't be too liberal. An employee should never be defining his own job completely. Keep your guidelines and objectives strong and specific, and communicate them to your staff. If you create a condition of freedom within limitations, you will motivate your employees while still holding control over your operation.

Here are a few motivating phrases you can use:

> "Take a look at this more carefully, then tell me how you intend to handle it."
>
> "See if you can find a way to get this done faster."
>
> "How would you approach a job like this?"

Finally assure your employees of your faith in them and your interest in the project. A simple phrase like "This is a big job, and I'm sure you'll do great things with it" can work wonders. Remember, delegation not only saves you a little time, it also creates pride and satisfaction in your staff and family members.

STEP SIX: *Monitor the Employee's Progress.*

Setting a schedule for evaluating the progress of delegated work is a tricky business. If you check too often, you're starting to waste your own time again on work you delegated. If, on the other hand, you don't take a look at things from time to time, you are inviting disaster.

The checkpoint schedule for every project will probably be different. It depends on the difficulty of the job, its priority level, the abilities of the employee, and the amount of time it will take to complete the task.

If the work is difficult and holds a high priority, you should be checking its progress often. A few moments each day or two might be enough to insure success without wasting time. A project like this will often have built-in break points, when one phase is completed and another begins. These stop-start moments may be the perfect time to evaluate progress.

Whenever you give a difficult job to a less experienced employee or child, whether from necessity or from a desire to train, frequent checking is essential. You may want to double the rate of evaluation for this employee. And be certain to offer an open ear to the worker. Let him know you are interested and ready to discuss any major problems or questions.

Generally, for relatively simple projects delegated to employees you are certain can handle the work, weekly check-ups should suffice. But again, allow the employee the freedom to come to you with problems, while at the same time discourage needless interruptions.

The method of progress evaluation should be clear. Ask the employee to tell you what he has done so far. Get an estimate of how much work remains. Ask him to tell you about any problems he's run into or improvements he's made. And finally, get a hard and fast answer about your deadline and the chances for making it. Force the employee to commit himself to a time and date.

STEP SEVEN: *Review and Evaluate Your Success.*

When the delegated project is finished, it is time to evaluate your effective delegation system. This should be a team effort in which your employees comment and criticize their own performance on the project. You may wish to do this in writing first and then hold a short meeting to discuss the written evaluation. (With family members, the evaluation can easily take place during the dinner hour.)

But first, ask yourself these questions. Was the project completed on time? Were the objectives of the project fulfilled? Did the employee create a new way of handling work like this? Has the employee learned anything or gotten any benefit from this experience?

With these questions as the basis of your evaluation, invite your employees to comment. So many times, the most accurate appraisals and toughest criticisms come from the employees themselves. They're the ones who accomplished the tasks, and they may be more qualified to evaluate it than you are.

The evaluation process will take some time. But as your effective delegation system grows and matures, you will find yourself investing less and less time in evaluation. The system will run itself.

As you evaluate, consider not only the objectives and time deadlines of the project, but also the degree of motivation in the helper. Try to sense how excited or inspired he was by the work. Use your impressions here to form new concepts about the employee and to change the nature of the work you delegate to him or her.

One vital aspect of the evaluation process is the creation and presentation of rewards. How should you reward an assistant for a job well done? All too often, executives "reward" good workers with tons of work. This person has proved he can do it, so why not let him handle more? This idea seems fine in principle, but in practice it is greatly abused. If a competent, responsible employee feels his only reward for success will be a greatly increased work load, he may find it hard to get motivated —

especially if he is doing twice the work of other employees without twice the money.

New responsibility and respect are rewards; burdensome work load is not. Even your personal confidence is a great reward and motivator. You may wish to tell them a little something about yourself — your problems with superiors, your objections, criticism or comments on other work-related things. This kind of "inside information" shows trust and respect for the employee and will encourage him to keep working successfully and efficiently.

Finally, look for developing patterns in your delegation system. Select those aspects you'd like to repeat and eliminate the procedures you find inefficient. While freedom and change are motivators, so is a certain degree of security and consistency. Your employee will be happy to know what you are pleased with and what you'd like to see changed.

If your delegation system is working well, everyone is benefitting from it. If something is going wrong, look for these two major pitfalls many executives overlook:

The Rolls Royce Syndrome. This is perfectionism again, but now it is extrapolated from oneself to one's employees. Perfectionism is negative delaying — it wastes time and effort. Criticizing employees because a project did not work out perfectly, or encouraging them to muddle over a project in search of genius is bad delegation. After all, you need the job done well. Such tactics only encourage poor performance.

Emotional Attachment. As I said earlier, emotional ties in work are destructive. You might be placing too much emotional value — positive or negative — on the work you delegated. Or the employee may be getting too involved in the work — fearing failure and desiring perfection unnecessarily. Either way, the result is a loss of perspective, wasted energy, and a poor working system.

Your Effective Delegation System, if properly established, should have each of the following characteristics:

1. The project is clearly defined.
2. The problems involved and results desired are fully understood by you, and the employee.
3. Guidelines are created within which the employee can execute the job in his or her personal style.
4. The helper has the proper knowledge, skill, and authority to handle the job.
5. The task is a source of training and education for the employee.
6. The task relates directly to your priorities and goals, and it is worthwhile.

If a delegated project has run into major problems, either due to employee mistakes or outside forces, your behavior and reaction to the problem will be critical. If you handle the problem intelligently, you are setting an example of good executive behavior for your staff. If you blow your top, you will create a poor morale among your helpers.

When a problem arises, pause and listen. And remember; don't correct the problem yourself. That is part of the project and the responsibility of the employee. Everyone has the right to make mistakes, and the duty to correct them.

In time, you may find it quite easy to create a system in which your employees themselves delegate work to other staff people below them. The essential element here is your example. If you've been a good delegator, chances are your employees will be, too. Be sure they understand that the chain of responsibility passes through them to whomever winds up handling the work they delegate. Just because they pass some portion of a project along to someone else does not mean they aren't responsible for its efficient completion. If the employee is bright, he or she will take his example from you and begin to use the same methods of communication and motivation you do.

It may be wise to create a delegation file or list: a fully detailed account of the projects currently in your department which should be handled by someone besides you. This file could be two-part: one list of jobs to be delegated by you and a second list of projects to be delegated by your employees. Such a list, if it is clearly created and accessible to everyone, will help conquer your communication problem.

In the long run, delegation will save you time in a number of ways. You will have established a routine which will become easier to use and more polished and efficient with each passing month. You will be freed from all the routine tasks which have wasted your time and left your staff sitting idle. You will have cultivated the talents and creativity of your staff and made them capable of doing more work more productively. Your department will have become more active, more productive and more profitable. But should you find problems still surfacing in your delegation system, use the following delegation checklist to uncover them. Then correct them immediately. Each of these questions relates to a delegation problem. Either you aren't delegating enough, or you are doing something incorrectly.

Chances are, if you answer yes to more than three of these questions, you have not created an Effective Delegation system. If not, go back to the beginning of this chapter and try again. (See *Delegation Checklist* opposite.)

Rate yourself on this checklist. If you answered affirmatively to more than three questions, re-evaluate your own talent as an executive delegator.

One final warning: Beware of upward delegation. Usually, work is delegated down the corporate ladder, to people who earn less money and have less experience. But often, employees discover they can delegate work back up to you. A common phrase they use is ''I'd like your opinion on this,'' or ''With

---

Delegation Checklist

1. Do you frequently take work home with you?
2. Do you work longer hours than your employees?
3. Do you spend time on your subordinates' work when no major problems exist?
4. When you return from a trip, is your "IN" basket always filled?
5. Are you still performing tasks that relate to your first job in this company?
6. Are you often interrupted for information about delegated projects — information the employee should have found on his or her own?
7. Do you spend valuable time on routine activities others could do?
8. Do you retain a participatory role in delegated projects, performing tasks the employee should handle?
9. Do you have to rush to meet deadlines?
10. Are your priorities determined essentially by urgency or emergency?
11. Have you been forced to skip vacations?
12. Do you receive many business-related phone calls at home?
13. Do you lack time for outside interests and pursuits?

---

your experience and know-how, would you handle the project this way?" The common result is that you wind up doing the work. If this kind of backwards delegation is going on in your department, stop it immediately and replace it with an Effective Delegation system.

8

Do It

If it were done when tis done, then 't were well
It were done quickly . . .

— Shakespeare

If you aren't a lover of Shakespearian drama, that quotation
may seem a little cryptic. In fact, its message is quite simple,
and its advice rather ingenious. The words are from Macbeth,
that well-known murderer from the Middle Ages. He's talking
about the act of assassination, and he wisely points out that if
you're going to complete a task, you should do it fast.

When it comes to work, the faster you can get a job done,
the better. Even if you are a workaholic (as I am), you still
don't want to spend any more time on a single job than is absolutely necessary. Naturally, you try to get things done quickly now. You don't deliberately dawdle or waste time on work
projects. You want to get matters taken care of and out of your
way as soon as possible. But in spite of your desire, this just
doesn't seem to happen in your life. Jobs tend to drag on
forever. Projects always take a lot longer than you anticipated.
You establish deadlines for yourself and your staff, and as
many times as not, the deadlines are broken.

Like all other ideas in the Hour Power program, effective
action is created when distinct and practical objectives and
guidelines exist.

Let's imagine you are about to take an automobile trip across some lonely western state you've never set foot in before. Besides your car and some gasoline, the most important tool for your journey is a good map. The map is your plan for this trip. It tells you where you are right now, and where you want to wind up. It shows you your goal and where you stand in relation to it.

The map also tells you exactly how you will get from here to there. It shows you step by step the method you will use to fulfill your goal.

During your trip, where do you keep your map? In the trunk? In a suitcase? Of course not. You keep the map beside you in the car so you can refer to it whenever you want to.

Getting through a work day, whether at home or in an office, is like traveling across that western state. You want to get from here to there: from breakfast to bedtime. And just as when traveling, you'd like to take the most direct route. Your map showed you the best highways and roads to take. You need the same kind of plan to get through your work day successfully.

In this chapter, I'll talk about forming a schedule for every work day of your life. This schedule will work exactly like a map. It will show you where you are, where you're trying to go, and exactly how to get there. And just as you keep your map in the front seat of the car, your schedule should be at your side, too, where you can find it quickly. If you lose your map — or your schedule — you won't go anywhere.

Have you ever heard of Parkinson's Law? It states that the amount of time a job takes will be equal to the amount of time available. In other words, if you've got the time to waste on a single project, you will. The same job then, can take two people two completely different amounts of time, depending on how much (or how little) pressure they feel to complete it quickly.

Your schedule is going to show you how to defeat Parkinson's Law. Through the objective use of priorities, deadlines, and efficient habits, you will find you can do more work in less time, and perhaps do the work better than before. The time you save is yours to use in any fashion — for extra work, play, or any reason at all.

But before you can begin to form your personal action schedule, you must set priorities for your work.

If you've put the first three of the Four D's (Drop, Delay, Delegate) to work in your life, you should already have a strong idea of what your priorities are. You've dropped the work that has no priority value at all. You delayed the projects that were incomplete or emotionally significant for you. And you've delegated most of the lower priority work to your assistants. What's still left is the work you yourself must DO — the last of the Four D's.

Of the projects you must do yourself, determine which are the most pressing or important and give these jobs the highest priority. You will do this work first, or during your peak performance work hours. The rest of the work must wait. Often, this delay is beneficial, because you may discover that even more of the lower-priority work can be delegated than you might have thought at first.

Once your priorities for any given day are set, you can begin to understand exactly where your time should be given. You can begin to get things done efficiently.

Deadlines are also extremely valuable for efficient work. In some professions, deadlines are an everyday fact of life. People who work for newspapers, for example, operate under constant deadlines. In less than 24 hours, they write, edit, organize, and print thousands upon thousands of words. The resulting product is a good, informative daily newspaper. The deadlines and pressures are heavy, but the work gets done, quickly and cheaply.

I suggest you create a personal deadline for every project you undertake. This deadline should be reasonable, but firm. It should make you aware of how you're using your time. Most of the executives I have worked with say that a strict deadline produces faster work in the vast majority of instances.

But before we go much farther on this road to productivity, let's talk about your attitude. Just like your helpers, you may need some motivation to get you going. I have a suggestion.

When your schedule is put into use, you will quickly notice that you are truly saving a large amount of time every day — perhaps as much as a half-hour or more. To motivate yourself to stay with the schedule system, why not use the time you save to get out of the office a little earlier and beat some of the rush hour traffic? Or give yourself a few extra minutes for lunch? Whatever your situation, try using your extra time for something you enjoy . . . something that will encourage you to stick with your new timesaving system.

In this book, we have already seen many examples of how wasting time can become a habit. Now I want to talk about a few productivity habits you can develop to help you DO things better and faster. Once acquired, these good work habits will be a regular part of your behavior . . . like the position you sleep in, or the way to comb your hair.

The first productivity habit you should develop is getting an early start. I simply cannot say enough about the potential benefits of getting out of bed a few minutes earlier in the morning. From avoiding traffic jams to handling unexpected problems, just 15 extra minutes in your day can make a tremendous difference.

The first few days of getting up early may not be pleasant — and night owls may wish to modify this habit somewhat. You are likely to feel that starting early is more of a punishment than a benefit to you. But in time, you will begin to see just how much more work you are getting done and how much leisure time you are creating by sleeping a little less. In the beginning, though, you will need motivation. For the first week or two, use your extra morning time to make your day more pleasant. Sit and read the paper for 15 minutes, or have an extra cup of coffee. Soon, getting up early will become a habit, and the rewards can be replaced by more efficient uses of your time.

The second major productivity habit is clock watching. If you want to get hold of your time, you must be aware of what time it is. If you don't wear a watch, get one immediately, preferably with a built-in alarm. Be aware of when you start projects, how long they are taking in relation to how much work is getting done, and exactly when the project is completed. Keep notes during every working day of when different activities begin and end. If you do not keep an eye on the time, your schedule and deadlines will have no positive effect on productivity.

A third productivity habit deals with how you actually function at your desk. While working on any specific job, be sure you have all the related material right in front of you. If you have to get up for some paperwork from the filing cabinet, you are wasting time and inviting interruptions. Keep all elements of the project nearby, where you can reach them easily.

Also, be sure to get all unrelated material away from your desk. Notes or memos about other problems and projects will only serve to distract you from what you're doing now. On the other hand, by putting all the elements of the job you're doing right in front of you, you remind yourself to stick with this project until it's completed.

Another productivity habit is, as we've mentioned before, to delegate all work at the same time, preferably at the end of the day. This lets your employees know what they will be doing tomorrow, and prevents you from having to stop and delegate several times throughout the day.

Exactly how you handle work — the steps you take and patterns you follow — should also be habit. For example, do you start by writing out your plan of action? Do you form an outline of how this project will be handled? Writing this kind of step-by-step plan can help you organize your work time and use it well.

Some people like to attack the biggest parts of a project first. They jump right in and begin handling the largest problems. Other people like to begin with smaller details and build up to the major aspects of the job. Every person has a unique style of working, and different approaches produce the best results in different people.

Exactly how you work is up to you. Your personal style is what makes the Hour Power system unique and individual for everyone who uses it. I cannot tell you exactly how to work. All I can do is suggest you analyze your working style. Be experimental. Try new approachs, and see if your efficiency increases. The key here is flexibility. While your present method of working may be an old hard-to-break habit, it may not be optimal. If you hesitate to experiment, try the new methods first with lower priority work and see what happens. You may discover that you've been doing things wrong all your career.

When you find the best working methods for you . . . or even if you decide not to change your style of action . . . make the way you work a habit. Follow the same steps every time you can. Just like the concepts of the Hour Power Program, when you put a system to work and stick with it, it will eventually become easier to follow.

One work habit to break immediately is perfectionism. You have already seen how this obsessive behavior, applauded by some, is actually a form of procrastination. Remember: you are working, not painting the Mona Lisa. Get the job done and get it out of the office fast. In general, you need the work done well . . . but not to perfection. Unless you are among the idle rich, you simply cannot afford to be perfect. When you spend days and weeks on one job, working and reworking, you are not striving for perfection as much as you are fulfilling Parkinson's Law.

So far, you have determined which projects you must do yourself. The other jobs have been delegated, delayed, or dropped. With the above productivity habits in mind, it is now time to begin forming your schedule.

Remember, your schedule is your plan for the day. The best possible time to plan your daily schedule is actually the day before. By creating tomorrow's schedule this afternoon, you can take advantage of what I previously mentioned as "seasoning."

Say it's the last thing in the afternoon. Your employees have just left your office after a delegation session. You now have a list of the jobs you cannot drop, delay or delegate and therefore must do on your own. List all these projects on a piece of paper.

Now consider the importance of each job. Which has an early deadline? Are any already overdue? Which have been given to you by a superior? Which projects, if completed successfully, would reflect best on your department? Ask these questions, and you will find the priority levels of the work you must do. Now, assign each job a priority level numerically, the most pressing job is number one, the next most important number two, and so on.

By making these decisions this afternoon, you give yourself all night to reconsider. The determinations you made have time to sink into your brain. This is the "seasoning" I mentioned. And the chances are that as you mull over your priorities, you will discover some project that can be delegated.

Let's say, when you think about it, you realize your number five priority project can be handled by any staff member. So instead of doing this job yourself tomorrow, you delegate it to an assistant. Thus, you have saved more time, time you can use for higher priority jobs. Note, that if you had formed your schedule in the morning, you might have gone ahead and done job number five on your own. But by forming your work chart the day before, you gave it time to "season," and you found an additional timesaver.

When you have your list of priorities, you can begin to draw your schedule. The basic format should look like this:

Daily Work Schedule = By Category

	EVERYDAY	MUST-DO'S	PROJECTS	NON-WORK
6:00				
7:00				
8:00				
9:00				
9:30				
10:00				
10:30				
11:00				
11:30				
12:00				
12:30				
1:00				
1:30				
2:00				
2:30				
3:00				
3:30				
4:00				
4:30				
5:00				
6:00				
Evening				

Notice that I've created four categories for activity: Everyday, Must-Do, Projects, and Non-work. "Everyday" activities are those things you must do each and every day, and which should have a space reserved in your schedule. Examples of everyday actions include phone calls, reading mail, delegation sessions, planning the next day's schedule, and thinking. Thinking — in a prearranged period of time provided exclusively for this activity — should be an everyday job for you. We'll talk more about thinking as a time-saver in the next chapter. For now, just provide yourself with some time to think.

You may have other everyday activities, and these should be listed in your schedule as well.

Under "Must-Do's", enter all the demands on your time tomorrow that cannot be avoided. These include appointments, meetings, luncheons, or any other pursuit that you cannot drop. These activities will keep you from getting your priority work done, but if you work them into your schedule, at least you know how long they will take and how much time you'll have left over.

Under the category "Projects", you will enter all the work you yourself must do tomorrow. You should assign time to these jobs according to their priority, which you have already established, the higher priority tasks taking a more important place in your day. And each project should be given a predetermined amount of time, thus creating a self-induced deadline for all your work.

The last category is "Non-work," and this should include any projects or activities you have planned that do not relate to your job. From a leisurely lunch to a cocktail party, enter non-work activities in this category.

Now, let's start filling in your schedule. First, the everyday items can be entered. Second, enter "Must-Do's" — appointments, meetings, etc. Third, enter your "Do" projects, in order of priority. Finally, include non-work items (such as lunch). Perhaps your schedule will now look like this:

Daily Work Schedule = By Category

	EVERYDAY	MUST-DO'S	PROJECTS	NON-WORK
6:00				
7:00				
8:00	Thinking			
9:00	Mail			
9:30	Phone			
10:00		Appt. with Client		
10:30				
11:00			Project #1	
11:30				
12:00				
12:30				Lunch
1:00				
1:30				
2:00		Meet editor		
2:30			Project #2	
3:00				
3:30				
4:00	Delegate			
4:30	Schedule			

As you work on your high priority projects, be sure to implement all the productivity habits we discussed earlier. Concentrate only on the job at hand, avoiding all interruptions and distractions as much as possible.

You can schedule your entire day in this fashion. You should enter the time you awake and your commutation under "Non-work." If you have any social events coming up, enter these here, too. Your "Everyday" items should essentially be scheduled at the same times, but if a "Must-Do" interferes, you may have to adjust this part of the schedule from time to time.

The major advantage of this schedule is that it remains flexible and easy to use while also categorizing your activities and helping you stick to deadlines. When you can see how your time is being used, you can make changes and shifts — adapt to sudden problems and crises — while still retaining control over your time.

When selecting times for priority projects, keep your personality in mind. I usually recommend the top work be done first thing, as soon as possible. But some people are "off" in the morning, or more efficient in the afternoon, and therefore top priority work might be better left for these hours. When you do your top priority work is, again, a decision only you can make. Your style of work, your peak performance hours are unique and individual. But to be sure you really know when you work best, try some experimentation. For a few days, try doing top level work at different times of the day, and see when you are able to stay the closest to your self-imposed deadlines.

One problem many executives experience is over-scheduling. They plan too many projects and activities for one day. If you are setting realistic deadlines for your work, you should be able to avoid this pitfall of the overachiever. But still, there will be a tendency to feel you could still be getting more done. While this might be true, it probably isn't if you are scheduling correctly. Remember: trying to do too much is a major time waster. When you try to do everything for everyone, you wind up getting nothing done at all. So don't try to cram too many items into your schedule. Be simple and straight-forward, giving each project the time it needs — no more, and no less.

If you run into a problem that suddenly demands all of your time, your schedule is likely to go out the window. Don't let this bother you. It happens all the time. But also, don't let yourself get too far away from your schedule. Always return to it, even in crisis, and keep it up to date. The crisis that breaks your schedule today can wind up destroying it tomorrow as well if you don't keep things organized on paper.

Never allow yourself to leave work in the afternoon without a schedule for tomorrow. Even if the schedule is likely to be overturned by 9:00 A.M., have it ready anyway. Without it, you will be lost.

With your schedule in good working order, you have a handle on your day. But what about next week, next month or even next year? Is there some way to save time by scheduling in advance?

I've designed a calendar that is rather unique. For one thing, it is not laid out in one-week sections like most calendars. Instead, a full month is laid out on one line. And the calendar reads from bottom to top, unlike conventional calendars. My calendar has another unique quality: it's more than a year long. The calendar is designed like a wall poster, and it's about five feet tall.

Thus, if you begin using the calendar in January, your first entries are at the bottom of the page. Let's say you make an entry for January 10. Directly above this box is February 10, March 10, and so on, all the way to January 10 of next year.

The purpose of this calendar is not to note meetings and appointments; it is to set goals and measure productivity. Let's suppose that on January 10 you noted on the calendar that a new project has just come into your office. By February 10, you may be noting that the project is completed. You know exactly how long the work took.

You can use this concept in reverse. Suppose you noted the arrival of that project on January 10, and then entered ahead of time "project complete" on February 10. You are actually setting a deadline for the project, and this calendar will remind you to keep it.

In addition, the expanded nature of this calendar makes it useful for long-term evaluation. Next year, when you are making the final entries on this calendar, you can look back and see exactly how far you have come in the year gone by. You can analyze your progress, see how your department is doing in the long run, and evaluate the performance of your staff.

All the same benefits can be gotten from a regular calendar; mine is just easier to use. Its "one-page" format makes all the information available at a glance and saves the time of turning calendar pages. But you can use any calendar in the same way. The secret is to keep looking ahead and looking behind. See how far you've gone in the last week, the last month. Skip ahead in your calendar to note deadlines you want to impose. Note major activities and problems on the calendar instead of minor appointments and phone calls. Save the fine details for your schedule.

A calendar is really a tool for long-range time saving. It lets you look at a full year or more of your life in a few short moments. But people don't use calendars to their full potential. They concentrate on one or two weeks at a time, instead of using the calendar to measure and forecast the past and future.

Start using your calendar as a time-saving tool. Look at it every day. Feel free to note any comments or feelings you have about how business is going. Then review these ideas later on, and see if the status has changed. And always mark long-term goals and deadlines on the forthcoming calendar pages to remind yourself of what you should be accomplishing.

Schedules and calendars are time-saving tools. By showing you where your time is going, they open the door for you to save time and get more done. While many people feel enslaved by schedules and charts, they really are a source of freedom.

If you can't drop, delay, or delegate a project, you are forced to do it yourself. You can do it right — and fast — if you set priorities, impose deadlines, develop productive habits and form a tight working schedule. Without a plan for work, you may accomplish absolutely nothing at all.

There really is enough time to do the jobs you are responsible for and still enjoy leisure pursuits. It's simply a matter of knowing where you're wasting time today, and where you can save it tomorrow.

9

Time to Think

Though man a thinking being defined,
Few use the grand prerogative of mind.

— Jane Taylor

In this second section of the Hour Power Program, we will look at some of the day-in and day-out activities that most people can take for granted but which can be robbing you of the time you have in this life. We'll see how you can evaluate the minor details and find points of your behavior to discover how you can get more from the time you have, and even how to multiply and increase your time significantly.

These basic living skills should be practiced in unison with a strong system of goals, objectives and priorities, and within the Four D system you've learned. The first major living skill we will examine is the way we think.

As an executive or homemaker, it's your job to think. Management, whether of a house or a business, is thinking under another name. Your company pays you for what you know, and you pay others for their knowledge as well. I am reminded of the story of the plumber and the lawyer. The lawyer was having trouble for his sink, so he called the plumber. The plumber no sooner entered the room than he picked up a wrench, banged a few pipes, and begin to leave. "It's fixed," the plumber said. "Wonderful," replied the lawyer. "How much do I owe you?" "Fifty dollars," answered the plumber. "Fifty dollars for five minutes work? Are you crazy? How do you itemize a bill like that?" cried the lawyer. The plumber smiled and said, "Five dollars for banging pipes. Forty-five dollars for knowing where to bang."

In any position of responsibility, you are paid to think. Whether you are a small, independent businessman or a department chairman, the most profitable and beneficial thing you can do for your company is to think of ways to improve the system. And if you own a home, the best thing you can do is to think of ways to run it better.

If you come up with just one interesting idea each week for improving operations, you are earning your keep.

What's the potential value of one good idea? How much is it worth in dollars and cents? There is no single answer to this question. Consider the man who invented the wheel. How much has mankind gained from his moment of inspiration? How much time has the wheel saved in the last few thousand years?

The fact is that one simple idea can be worth a fortune. And a combination of ideas can change the world. If Thomas Edison had somehow maintained exclusive ownership of all the products that resulted from his ideas — including electric lights, phonographs, and movie cameras — how much would his total worth be? Such a figure is almost too great to ponder.

But it is not only the great inventions that qualify as profitable thought. Every time you come up with an idea to improve operations, you are saving time and making money. In your small way, you have made a breakthrough. And it all comes from the simple process of thought.

Suppose there's one project your staff handles each and every month — billing, perhaps. Now imagine you come upon an idea that cuts the time spent on billing dramatically. Say you can use this new idea to get your bills out a day earlier — with a day less work. Your little idea has saved one eight-hour day each month. Twelve full days in a year. That's more than two full working weeks added to your business year. How much can you and your staff accomplish in twelve extra days?

The concept of our discussion of thinking is two-fold: first, we will try to improve HOW you think, the actual mental process of problem solving. Then we'll talk about what you DO with your ideas — how you use them, lose them, and often confuse them.

Try as you may, you cannot make your mind function like a computer. And you probably wouldn't want to. The way you think, the thoughts that pop in and out of your consciousness, are what constitute your personality. Your individual style is the most important thing you possess. It's gotten you where you are today, and it will probably get you a lot further. It's really not to your advantage to change your mentality or the way you think. But it is beneficial to learn to organize your thoughts and ideas so they can be used.

What you need is a thinking system. A routine to follow, a pattern to trace, that will lead to clear, crisp, logical problem solving. As you may have guessed by now, I've got a system in mind.

Like the Four D's, the major thrust of this thinking system is forming objectives and evaluating actions. Just as you've learned to improve productivity and efficiency through scheduling and making lists and charts, you will use notation to improve your thinking.

Solving any problem is merely a matter of asking three simple questions: What's the problem? What is the cause? What are possible solutions? Now you're saying to yourself, "I ask those questions in my head. This is no great revelation." Stop and think again. Remember back before you began this book, how you thought you were saving time, working efficiently, making the most of your day? Lots of things in this life seem simple and straightforward, until you stop and objectively analyze them.

You may think you ask yourself these questions in problem solving, but do you really express them fully and in the proper sequence? I have observed that many people, when presented with a problem, start suggesting solutions before they've even determined what the problem really is. As the odds would have it, the solutions are sometimes correct. But more often, they do not even address the dilemma.

The next time you've got a problem to solve, take out a piece of paper and a pencil. Ask yourself each of the above questions and make a note of your answer. Try this just once and see if it doesn't lead to more thorough problem solving right away.

To reiterate, ask yourself "What is the problem?" Treat this question like you were adding fractions: look for the lowest common denominator. For example, if one member of your staff has been performing poorly lately, don't list your problems as "poor staff performance," or "my staff is unmotivated." Be specific! Your problem is one staff member who is not producing, so say "Frank is not performing as expected." That is really your problem, so write it down on your piece of paper.

Next, try to find the cause of the problem. This will be more difficult than question one, since many factors could be the root of your trouble. The wisest way to handle this question is to list several probable answers. Staying with the same question about Frank, you might find causes like "Expectations too high," "Frank lacks motivation," "Set up of operations is denying Frank incentives," and "Frank ill-chosen for his position." All of these and many other factors might be the cause of Frank's poor productivity. As you list all the possible causes, analyze them carefully. Some can probably be rejected right away. But keep all the logical causes on your list, and get ready to take action on each of them.

Now, ask question three: "How can I solve this problem?" Because you have several possible causes for Frank's problem, you will also have several possible solutions and each may be correct. On your list, give a possible solution for each of the likely causes you chose. Your list may now look like this:

1. PROBLEM: Frank not producing.

2. CAUSES: a. Expectations too high.
              b. Lack motivation.
              c. Not given incentives.
              d. Frank is ill-chosen.

3. SOLUTIONS: a. Adjust my expectations.
              b. Talk to Frank about his goals.
              c. Try adding more incentive.
              d. Replace Frank.

Each of these may be the answer to your problem. Until you examine the situation further, you really can't know for sure. But if you hadn't followed this system, you may have rashly fired Frank off hand, or you might have shuffled him around your staff until you found the place where he would do the least damage.

But within this list, you can proceed to objectively analyze the situation. For example, you may go back to the answers to question three and consider the validity of each. Should you re-evaluate your expectations of Frank? Perhaps not. Chances are your expectations and demands on him are quite reasonable, maybe even a little charitable. The job can be done with the right person, so it isn't your expectations that need to change. It's Frank.

Your second solution might be unacceptable, too. Frank's personal motivation and drive may not be your concern. Or maybe you feel you should not be bothered with other people's personal weaknesses. This sounds harsh, but it can be perfectly legitimate for a busy executive.

Now you're down to two possible solutions, and both seem valid. Either give Frank a little incentive and see if his productivity goes up, or get rid of him soon. The best bet would probably be to try the incentive first and keep the ax in the closet for a while.

This example may seem a bit simplistic, and perhaps it is, but when you apply this system to major corporate problems, or troublesome items at home, it begins to work wonders. Let's say you are running a million-dollar operation, and a client has threatened a lawsuit. Would you try to solve a problem like this off the top of your head? Of course not. You'd go through lengthly meetings, exchange lots of paperwork, and call in your top advisors. So why not handle everyday problems in a similar, organized fashion? Again, I urge you to just try writing down these three questions and answering each as I have shown with one problem in these days ahead. I am sure that after one try, you'll realize that your thinking and problem solving has been unorganized to date and is in need of improvement.

As you experiment and try to isolate possible causes and solutions of problems, be critical of your own ideas. In fact, it is always useful to second-guess yourself. If an idea doesn't work, throw it out. Too many people seem to hang on to old, unworkable ideas long after they have been proven false. Dropping ideas is just as important as dropping valueless work. Perhaps even more important. How many major American companies have gone under because they would not update their product line, or change their sales approach or find a new advertising agency?

Change is vital to success. You must be ready and willing to change and adjust when you need to. Essentially, you are responsible not only to accept this kind of change, you really should be implementing it. Those great new ideas that boost profits and shake up the industry really should be coming from your desk.

And chances are you have lots of ground-breaking ideas like that already. They probably come to you at odd hours, and in unusual places. You're sitting up late watching television, when suddenly a thought occurs: "What if we change the filing system?" Or you're lying on the beach on vacation when suddenly you have a nagging thought about the office: "What if I put Meyer in charge of purchasing?" But then, after a moment the thought fades away. Maybe the movie gets interesting, or you get up to put on some tanning lotion, and before you know it, that profitable notion is less than a memory.

Maybe you've gotten into the habit of jotting down thoughts on matchbooks and napkins. We've all heard the stories about great writers who compose beautiful works on the backs of envelopes. So when a great idea hits, you reach for anything that will take ink and try to make a note to yourself. But maybe you can't find a pencil, and the idea slips away. Or even worse, you jot down a lovely idea, put the paper in your pocket, and send the jacket to the dry cleaner. Goodbye to another brainstorm.

But there's one thing that's even more frustrating. You get a great idea in the middle of the night. You leap out of bed, jot down your thought and place the paper in your briefcase so you won't lose it. Tomorrow at work, you look at that little slip of paper and it says "E no good, FRD. to PD." You sit and stare at the message you made to yourself and wonder "What the hell does it mean?" A great idea, sitting right in the palm of your hand, and you can't make sense of it. This has got to be one of the most frustrating experiences there is.

I have a system that can prevent you from ever losing a brilliant flash of genius again. It's called the "Idea File and

Ledger System,'' and it might just bring you higher profits, greater efficiency, and a certain amount of fame in your field.

The process is simple: Write down every idea you have and file it. The first step is to dedicate a little drawer space to your idea file. This is where all your notations will go.

Next, make it a regular habit to carry pencil and paper with you at all times. I find it most useful to have one of those small note pads with a pencil attached.

From now on, whenever you have a thought about working operations and how they might be improved, write it down on a sheet of your pad. There are three items you should enter on the notation. First, record the time and place when the idea occurred to you. You can refer to this later when you review your idea file, and the time and place will make all the details and circumstances of your idea come back to you more clearly.

Second, write down the idea itself. Never use any form of code in your thought notations, since you may not interpret it correctly later on. Write in full sentences, and complete thoughts, and you will have no problem understanding the note later on.

Finally write something down about what this idea is intended to do. In other words, make a note of how you can benefit from this idea. This final note will not only help you remember the point of your thought, it will also help you keep lots of bad ideas out of your file. When you ask this third question, many ideas will reveal themselves as impoverished right away, and you can drop them.

When you've noted these three items, put them into your filing system. The idea is now there for you to use as you wish. You cannot lose it, forget it, or misinterpret it.

There is one more step in the process, which is to enter each idea you have into a ledger. The benefit of this is that you can review all your recent ideas in a single glance. Why is this important if you have all your ideas in your file? What extra benefit does the ledger bring?

Most often, powerful ideas come to us in bits and pieces. A thought here, a pondering there. Big ideas come in little slices. But when the two or three points are combined, genius is created. You may look through your ledger and notice that ideas number 5, 18, and 21 seem to have something in common. As you consider the situation, you realize that the three ideas in combination produce a real breakthrough concept. The ledger is the tool that opens up this possiblity for you. You can look at all your current ideas at once, and the interrelation between them can be uncovered.

It's also a great idea to have every member of your staff build his or her own file and ledger. Then, you can have a weekly meeting to discuss and compare ideas. Many times, you will find that one thought you had will combine with an idea from Jack and another from Sue, and the total concept will be a real profit maker.

By organizing how you record your ideas and then discussing them openly at weekly meetings, you'll find a dynamic new communication flowing through your organization. Your employees will be anxious to attend these meetings, and they will be encouraged to think more about improving your department. The number of new concepts and operating procedures that are suggested in this situation are amazing. And you may discover that your staff is a lot brighter and more innovative than you ever dreamed.

Acting before you think can lead to lots of problems. But thinking after you act can be very valuable. By reflecting on your actions and experiences, you can find lots of great ideas for improving the way you do business. I call this "After Action Analysis." Let's say you and your staff have just finished a project for a major client. Each of you should sit down, in private, and reflect on the experience. Three questions should be asked.

First, "What went right on this job?" Since fewer things usually go right than wrong, it's wise to ask this question first and get it out of the way. For many people, the answer to the first question may simply be "We got the job done."

Next, ask "What went wrong?" This is the bulky question, and you'll get lots of replies from each staff member. From minor details about your operation to major complaints about the client and his staff, you'll find people have a large number of ideas about what went wrong.

Finally, ask "How can I improve this operation next time?" This is the question that will eliminate the lightweights. Everyone can find something bad to say, but not everyone can come up with an idea to improve things. However, your staff, and you, too, will have lots of ideas here. Note all your ideas for improving things, and discuss your after-action analysis forms in your next idea meeting. By comparing and evaluating everyone's suggestions for improving operations, you may find business with that client going more smoothly next time around.

One note about your staff idea meetings: it's essential that your employees feel free to discuss and compare ideas, and one vital element here is that they feel they can disagree with you. If you tend to be insulted or upset when someone points out weak areas in your ideas, your staff will simply say yes to everything you suggest and no real knowledge will be achieved. Encourage your staff to second-guess and question you, and do the same to them. Be sure everyone understands that this is a cooperative effort, not a competition or personality struggle.

After Action Analysis can have many benefits for your organization. First, it will lead to easier operations in the future. Second, you may find through After Action Analysis that more work can be delegated to your staff. When your employees know how you think, what problems you have, and what your goals are, they become more capable of taking work off your hands and doing it themselves. Your After Action Analysis forms should also be filed, as they can be of great help in the future. Should you replace a staff member, or take on new help, these people can use the After Action Analysis forms for training purposes. They can learn quickly what you've done in the past and how you'd like to see things change. This is also true of the items in your idea file. Share this information with everyone who works with you.

So far, we've talked about thinking before you act and after an event is passed. But what about the present? Naturally, you are thinking all the time, before, during, and after you take action. But there may be a great time-saving, thinking system you are not taking advantage of.

It's the concept of getting two-for-one, three-for-one, or even four-for-one from everything you do. Throughout your day, no matter what you are doing, you should be looking for three- and four-for-ones.

Let's say you're in a meeting with a client. You should be asking yourself at every moment, "What more can I accomplish here?" For example, if you simply meet with the client and discuss one area of business, you get one-for-one. If you can also use this time to establish a personal or professional relationship with the client, you've got a two-for-one. If you also look out for potential problems that could be avoided next time, you are getting three-for-one. And if you ask the client about others he knows who might benefit from your services, you are getting a full four tasks accomplished where others may only succeed in doing one.

Thinking about three- and four-for-ones is the best way to find them. If you don't search them out, most timesavers are quite elusive. But when you are looking to save time — and thinking about it — you can begin to get more from your mind.

If you don't take the time to think about possible three- and four-for-ones, you will only get one-for-one . . . or maybe even less.

You'll recall in the last chapter we entered an item on your schedule simply called "thinking." This is an idea that I suggest to all the executives who seek my advice: provide a certain amount of time each day to think. Whether a few minutes in the morning, or at the end of the work day, or ultimately both — taking the time to think brings tremendous rewards.

During this Thinking Time, avoid all interruptions. This is the perfect opportunity to evaluate your idea ledger, undertake some after-action analysis, or just reflect on what you're doing, what you are about to do, and look out for potential problems that you may be able to side-step. If you can escape just one obstacle each day because you took the time to think about the problem first, you will be more productive and efficient immediately.

In the long run, the benefits of thinking right are almost too great to measure or describe. The possible improvements you can make, the breakthrough ideas you may create, the potential profits and saved time, all can come from thinking correctly and with an organized plan.

In today's tough business world, it's the innovator who gets ahead. More and more, the best managers are the ones who produce positive change, who create new systems and designs for working efficiently, who define the new ideas that soon become industry standard.

If you can learn to think within a set program, you will be able to harness the powers of your mind and put them to work for you.

One note: be sure you are the kind of executive who lets others think for themselves. If you hand out assignments and delegate work with tremendous amounts of explanation and instruction, you are discouraging your employees from bothering to think. Soon, they will hesitate to make any decision of their own. If, however, you say to your staff: "I'll let you figure this out," they will be inspired to use their own minds for productive purposes.

Finally, keep in mind that there is one excellent way to STOP thinking about work. Many career people find themselves drifting back to the unanswered problems and unaddressed projects of the day even when they are trying to relax. This can put a tremendous strain not only on the executive, but also on his family and friends.

The way to put work out of your mind is the psychological concept I mentioned before known as "closure." Under this principle, we see that the reason most people cannot stop thinking about work is that they have left so many things "open-ended." That is, so much business has been left undone, so many problems unsolved, that the executive simply cannot stop worrying about them.

If you're following my system, closure is already working for you. At the end of your day, you have either finished a job, or else you know exactly what you will do next with each project. You have a schedule that tells you their status, and you know just how you will handle them tomorrow. If your schedule is good, you can shut off the office light, walk away, and not bother to think about work until tomorrow morning. Your schedule provides closure.

10

Managing Interruptions

*How sweet, how passing sweet, is
solitude!*

— William Cowper

At times, it seems our lives are a series of interruptions.
Perhaps military service interrupted your career plans. Or a
brief illness interrupted your vacation plans. Interruptions are
a fact of modern life.

Remember Murphy's Law? "If anything can possibly go
wrong, it will. And at the least convenient time." If there's any
aspect of life to which Murphy's Law applies without exception, it is interruptions. Interruptions always occur when you
least expect them, when you are the least prepared for them,
and when they do the maximum amount of damage.

Our lives are interrupted constantly. At work, phone calls
and unexpected visits get in the way. Our travel is interrupted
by everything from traffic to flat tires to fog at the airport.
Even our favorite television programs are interrupted by
commercials.

You can almost say with dogmatic authority that if you want
to concentrate . . . if you want a little privacy or solitude . . .
something will interrupt you.

Exactly what happens when you are interrupted?

1. You stop what you are doing.

2. You start dealing with the interruption.
3. The interruption ends. You stop thinking about it.
4. You go back to what you were doing and start up again.

Stop-start. Stop-start. Every interruption in your life requires these four actions. With shorter interruptions, the shifting takes less time. But as the interruptions go up in duration, the amount of time needed to get back to what you were doing increases, too.

If you've been putting the principles of this book to work in your life, you know how time-consuming and distracting priority shifts can be. But every time you pick up the telephone, say hello to someone in the hallway, or pause to think about your personal problems or interests, you are shifting priorities. You are wasting time.

Unnecessary or poorly timed phone calls . . . questions from employees, small talk with friends . . . worries, doubts and fears . . . each and every one of these items and many more are preventing you from accomplishing your high priority activities. They are destroying your schedule, minimizing your productivity, and pushing you further and further away from your goals.

How can you eliminate those interruptions? Which are important, and which are meaningless? Is there some way to escape the wasted time and save the energy these interruptions require?

As with every other aspect of time management, the secret to changing and improving is evaluation. You must determine exactly what is interrupting you and then formulate a plan that will minimize these intrusions into your life.

Essentially, all interruptions can be categorized in two groups: external and internal. You are interrupted by external things like phone calls and visitors, and also by internal concerns like personal matters, anxieties, and guilt. All interruptions come either from other people or from yourself.

The first step in evaluating your interruptions is to undertake a "Selective Interruption Study." This is a relatively simple exercise, involving a little time and effort from you. But with the findings this study will provide, you can begin to understand the factors that interrupt you and form policies and plans to sidestep them as often as possible.

The principle involved in making a Selective Interruption Study is a simple one: you merely record all the things that force you to shift priorities. This should include internal as well as external interruptions, from your fellow executives who stop by to chat to the little daydreams that come and go every few minutes.

It is vital to the best formation of your study that you consider a time period beyond one single day. For best results, record your interruptions for two or three days consecutively; the time each occurred; the nature of each interruption; and the duration of each.

Then, synthesize your interruption record with your priority schedule. First, determine from your priority schedule what business you wish to undertake today. On a sheet of paper, list the date, your high priority work, and the time you intend to begin. The chart should look like this:

Major Project	Start Time	Max. Time Needed
Job X	9:00	2 hrs.

Note that you have also listed an objective estimate of how long that job should take. Be sure this estimate reflects a reasonable degree of efficiency, without extra time for interruptions. Don't make your estimate indicate how long such a project normally DOES take you. Instead, let it show you how long the job SHOULD take you.

Now, begin listing all your interruptions, noting when they began, what they concerned, and when they stopped. Your chart may now look like this:

Interruptions:

Start	Nature	Stop
1. 9:10	phone: Fred says hi.	9:15
2. 9:23	phone: Phil reminds me of meeting.	9:30
3. 9:45	visit: Secy. has a question.	9:47
4. 10:05	me: pause to worry about Job Y.	10:10

(While our sample chart concerns office work, homemakers should create their chart in the same fashion.) You are recording all forms of interruption, external and internal. You should continue listing interruptions til Job X is completed. Then note the time when you finished the job and how long it actually took you.

Major Project	Finish Time	Time Used
Job X	12:25	3.25 hrs.

Now indicate the next major project you will begin, again based on your priority schedule. List the time you will start working on this activity, and again objectively estimate how long it should take you without interruptions. Avoid the temptation to scale up your estimate based on this morning's disappointing showing. List also any activities that occur between priority projects.

Lunch — 12:25 to 1:30

Major Project	Start Time	Max. Time Needed
Job Y	1:30	3 hrs.

Now again begin listing your interruptions and continue until Job Y is completed. Note the start time, nature, and stop time of all interruptions, and the actual time taken to complete the job.

At the end of the day, review your Selective Interruption Study. The first thing to note is the disparity between your estimated time need for each project and the actual amount of time the project took to finish. In our sample study, Job X was given a maximum estimated time of two hours. The job actually took 3 hours and 25 minutes to complete.

The difference between these two times — in this case almost an hour and a half — is the amount of time you're losing to interruptions. The wasted time you notice in your first day of Selective Interruption Study should be more than enough to make you realize that interruptions are wasting your life, destroying your productivity, and keeping you from your goals.

I strongly urge you to continue your study for at least two more days, even longer if possible. When you've accumulated enough data about the things that interrupt you, you can begin to save time.

How can this study help you prevent interruptions? By showing you where your interruptions come from, when they tend to occur most often, and which are worth the time they take and which are simply wasteful.

Interpreting your Selective Interruption Study is a personal, subjective matter. I can help you get started by showing you the factors to look for. But ultimately, the decisions will be up to you. You will have to evaluate the importance of phone calls, conversations, and meetings. You'll have to make personal decisions about your schedule, work habits, and daily patterns. A fairly high amount of creative decision making is involved.

First examine your study for external interruptions: those work stoppers that come from other people. Count how many of them occurred in a typical day. Better still, count each day's total for the three day period you studied, then average them out for a single day's estimate. Note this number at the bottom of your study chart.

Next, add up the duration times of all external interruptions on each of the three days. (You can be a little rough with this number.) Add the three day totals together, divide by three, and you have an average external interruption time for a single day. Note this on your study chart, too.

The next step is to create an imaginary condition, a Utopia in which you get all your work done without pointless interruptions. You can do this by selecting a random percentage of your external interruptions that you'd like to avoid. For example, let's say on an average day you are interrupted a total of 30 times, for a duration of about 2 hours. By how much would you like to reduce this total? If you're dreaming about saving time, your answer should be 100%, but this simply is not possible. Many of those interruptions come from superiors or relate directly to high priority work. You just can't avoid such important interruptions.

But the fact is that important interruptions don't take much time. (Go over your study chart again and see if this isn't the case.) That important interruptions are usually short, and wasteful interruptions long, makes sense according to Murphy's Law. It also appeals to your common sense: if someone calls, drops by, or otherwise interrupts you about work matters, they are likely to want fast answers and not small talk. They will get the information they need and say goodbye.

We can see then that the longest interruptions are usually the least valuable. When people have nothing important to say, it takes them a long time to say it. They simply procrastinate, which is logical since they are probably interrupting you to avoid their own work anyway.

Therefore, the percentage of interruptions you'd ultimately like to avoid should be quite high. Perhaps not 100%, but 80% at least. The remaining 20% will be worthwhile interruptions, and will not take much time.

That's your objective: cut interruptions by 80%. So, we can say that in your fantasy world, 80% of the external things that now interrupt you would not exist. But how can you rid yourself of these time wasters? The solution is a three-step process: isolate the wasteful interruptions, discover their source, and determine when they tend to occur.

Using your study chart, create a list of interruptions that occurred in the last three days, placing the important interruptions in one column and the meaningless interruptions in a second. Now go through the record of your day, entering each interruption in one list or the other.

Determining which interruptions are worthwhile and which are not is far easier than it seems. Simply return to your goals and priorities. If an interruption relates directly to the accomplishment of a priority project or the achievement of a goal, it is important and should not be avoided. Examples of this kind of good interruption are calls from your boss, calls that provide needed information, important errands, visits from clients, and so on. If it helps you do your job or attain your goal, it's worth the stop-start time it takes.

All other interruptions are pointless and wasteful . . . friendly phone calls, chit-chat, questions from employees that don't really require your attention.

When you've got your list of negative information, it's time to start looking for patterns. See if there are two or three sources that create most of your wasteful external interruptions. You'll probably discover that a few specific individuals, or one or two general groups, are interrupting you all the time.

You may find that most of your interruptions are coming from a certain co-worker, your secretary, or one or two particular clients. Or on the other hand, your external interruptors may fall into groups: personal friends, associates, employees. Whether it's one individual or a group of people, you should determine where your interruptions are coming from.

Now you have a little "enemies" list: the names of those who are wasting your time and keeping you from getting things done. These are the people you must avoid.

The next question is "When do these people interrupt me?" Go back to your study chart and see if the interruptions are scattered around the day, or if they tend to pile up around a specific hour.

Now you know which interruptions are wasteful, who they come from, and when they come. But how can you put this information to use?

The best ways of avoiding phone calls, conversation in the office, meetings, and employee interruptions will be discussed in greater detail later in this chapter. Right now, there are two things you can do.

Give your secretary a list of all the external negative interruptors that bother you by phone. From this point forward, instruct her to hold all calls from these individuals with the exception of dire emergencies.

Your Selective Study is paying off already. You've probably just cut your number of interruptions in half.

The second step involves scheduling. Since you now know when during the day most of your negative external interruptions occur, you can prepare yourself for them. If they tend to occur when you've reserved low-priority work, your're ready for annoying interruptions to occur.

If they come during high-priority work, however, you have a problem. Optimally, you should be using your best hours for high priority work, and interruptions are particularly destructive here. The solution is not to schedule your work differently, but rather to do all you can to eliminate the interruptions, or at least delay them.

Many people have begun scheduling what are called "quiet hours." This idea simply means reserving one hour each day when no interruptions are permitted, except extreme emergencies. In order to establish your own quiet hour, you will have to do some publicity work. First, select the hour of the day when most of your negative external interruptions seem to take place. Declare this time your quiet hour. Inform all your associates, employees, clients, and friends that you are not available during this time. Be diplomatic, yet firm. Tell them that if you are to do the work they want correctly, you must have this one hour each day to yourself. And if they should forget and call you anyway, they will be less put off when your secretary says you're not available.

Quiet hours are one aspect of "planned unavailability." The exact scheduling of your quiet hour is a matter of personal judgment. In fact, you may find the entire concept unappealing. I suggest you give it a try for a few days and see if you don't change your mind.

The second form of negative interruption — internal — is in one way easier to handle, but in another way more difficult. Since these interruptions come from you, they can potentially be eliminated altogether. You can, theoretically, cut these internal interruptions by 100%. The problem is that these interruptions have psychological origins, and so may be harder to fight than phone calls.

Look again at your study chart. Examine each of the internal interruptions you listed. Why did you stop working? What were you daydreaming or worrying about? Were you just thinking about your weekend, or were you agonizing about your job security, longing for fulfillment, worrying about your marriage?

I can give you a few tips that will help you avoid these internal interruptions, or at least give you the time and flexibility to deal with them and not lose too much time.

The Night Before Plan. Each night, take a little time to prepare for tomorrow. As you should be doing now, set a schedule for the day to come. Know what you want to do, in what order, and you can avoid a lot of the guilt and anxiety that comes from worrying about which work should get done when. Use the Hour Power Four D system at all times when setting your working schedule.

Get An Early Start. I've mentioned it before, but I cannot say enough about getting out of bed earlier than you have to. It gives you the extra time you'll need to handle sudden problems. And it will encourage a relaxed mood that will help prevent internal interruptions.

Change Your Structures. Are you still walking around your office to get things that should be at your fingertips? Do you put anxiety-producing materials right in front of you on your desk, where they will interrupt you over and over again?

If you are using my program correctly, the system of goals and priorities should help you shake the self-interruption habit.

By this time, you've got a pretty good idea of where your interruptions come from. I hope you are beginning to attack some of the personal troubles that harm your working abilities. Right now, I'd like to tell you about fighting off the barrage of external interruptions you receive each day.

By giving your secretary a list of "don't bother me" callers and creating a quiet hour, you are well on your way to that 80% interruption reduction you dreamed of. But what about important phone calls? Can they be shortened further still? And how about wandering co-workers and neighbors who happen into your office or home during high-priority work? How can you "shoo" them away?

External interruptions, whether worthwhile or not, fall into three categories: phone calls, visits, and inquiries from employees. For each of these groups there are specific tricks that can cut down on interruption duration and often eliminate it altogether.

Let's begin with your employees. Naturally, the people who work for you will need your advice or assistance from time to time. Unfortunately, it often seems that the time they pick is the worst possible. Here's a checklist for stopping this kind of external interruption.

Delegate Right. If you give an employee all he needs to perform a delegated task, including information, tools, materials, etc., he or she should not need to interrupt you for additional advice. Double check your delegation technique, looking for omissions or mistakes you make that lead to further interruptions.

Evaluate the Employee. Some people will interrupt you for no reason at all. Perhaps they want to get your attention, to show you how hard they're working. Others may be looking to delegate work up to you. Still others are seeking a quick answer to a question they could solve on their own. If your employees are bothering you for any of these reasons, set them straight right away and you'll cut interruptions considerably.

Staff Meetings. It's a good idea to schedule staff meetings with your helpers for specific times every day or two. This will give your employees a chance to talk with you without causing an interruption. This idea seems simple, but most businessmen steadfastly refuse to schedule meetings with their employees. They prefer to handle questions and problems when they occur. This kind of seat-of-the-pants, crisis management leads directly to interruptions. Provide a specific time for communication with your staff and you'll be communicating effectively and efficiently without interruption.

Next, let's consider the telephone. While this device has changed our world, it has also eliminated privacy. In desperation, 16% of all Americans with phones have turned to unlisted telephone numbers. In Los Angeles, the rate of unlisted phones is 38%.

If you think you get interrupted by the phone a lot now, be prepared for even more time wasting tomorrow. Phone advertisers are becoming quite skillful at locating you — both at home and in the office — for their sales pitches. A computer has even been developed which will call up to 1,000 numbers each day and play a recorded promotional message when you answer!

The phone company is actively promoting a boom in telephone interruptions. Perhaps you've seen the commercial which claims a phone call is cheaper than a business letter. If people start using the phone for all their business correspondence, no one of us will ever get anything done. We'll spend the entire day answering and returning phone calls.

The best way to cut down on incoming calls is to have your secretary screen them. You've already given a list of multiple interruptors to her, so those calls will all be held. But it may be time to take a daring step.

Why not create a V.I.P. list — a group of names of those people whose calls you will always take. This list should include your immediate bosses, your spouse, your children if any, and a daily addition of the client whose work you're doing today.

Tell your secretary that any of these V.I.P.'s calls will be accepted. All other people should be held, except in an emergency. Give your secretary your priority schedule for the day. Show her the times when you don't want to be disturbed and have her use this V.I.P. system during those times.

How should your secretary get rid of these unimportant callers? With friends, the truth works best. Have her tell them you are very busy and you'll call back later. Any good friend will understand and not be offended.

With business associates and clients, the truth works worst. You don't ever want to tell a client you have more important work than his. So teach your secretary how to lie. The old tried-and-true phrases do just fine: "He's in a meeting," "He just stepped out of the office," and so on. Instruct her to vary the lies she uses so as to minimize caller aggravation and your obvious guilt. The caller knows you're probably not in a meeting, and he will accept the fact that you don't want to talk to him right now. But if your secretary tells him you're in a meeting twice a day, his intelligence will be insulted. Teach your secretary to lie with style and creativity.

You can also cut the duration of important, necessary phone interruptions. Do everything you can to lead the conversation to important matters and avoid small talk. A certain amount of tact is required, but with practice you'll find little ways to get them off the line without insulting anyone. (One great method is to create an imaginary "call on the other line" or "associate just stepped into my office.")

You can use your outgoing calls to minimize incoming calls, too. The secret is preparation. If you have to call Joe Smith about one subject, look for other important matters you can discuss at the same time. If you find just one more topic to discuss, you have effectively eliminated one interruption. The more business you discuss per phone call, the more interruptions you avoid later on.

It is also wise to cluster your outgoing phone calls. After your secretary has taken all those messages from those numerous interruptors, arrange a time during the day when you will return all these calls at once. Discuss as much as is useful in each call. And if you can't find someone (if he or she is "in a meeting"), don't tell them to call you back. Call again yourself, at your own chosen time, and still one more interruption is stopped. Grouping phone calls lets you get all your telephone business out of the way at once, while you are ready for it, instead of while you are trying to do high priority work.

If you've established a quiet hour, defend it to the end! Even the V.I.P.'s should wait until after it, unless a true crisis exists.

So far, you've cut interruptions and necessary phone calls. You may have noticed that managing interruptions relies heavily on the Four D's. You drop calls. You delay conversations. You delegate the power to interrupt to your secretary, with exact objectives and guidelines.

The few interruptions that remain, that absolutely cannot be dropped, delayed or delegated, are done. You accept them, lose a little time and move on.

In addition to your employees and your phone, the last category of interruptors are people who just want to chat. Associates may wander into your office to talk, or pour out the details of some crisis or emergency. The long conversations you get dragged into at the coffee machine, in the washroom, or in the hallways, have the same result: your time is wasted, your work interrupted.

If the interrupting associate is a friend, the truth is again your best defense. Whether they have wandered into your office or simply buttonholed you in the hall, tell them honestly that you have tons of work to do and would be happy to see them at lunch or after work. Again, a true friend will respect this.

But what if the visitor is not a friend? How do you handle these interruptors? The methods are a little sneaky. They require a good poker face and some cooperation from your staff.

One idea is to prevent the visitor from ever sitting down. The moment he walks in, jump up and grab his hand, shaking vigorously as you gently keep him standing. Remain standing yourself and pass a little small talk. Then before he sits, walk around the desk as though you are escorting him to the elevator. If you smile enough, you can get the visitor out of the room without insulting him. At times, the visitor will almost believe he never intended to sit down in the first place.

When a visitor plants himself in your office and refuses to leave, let your secretary in on the conspiracy. Create a code — something that sounds common but which you never use normally. This code should tell your secretary to come into the office and remind you of that urgent call you must return or the crisis project you should be working on. Most visitors will get the hint and be on their way shortly. (I told you this was sneaky.)

Ask yourself if you aren't actually inviting these interruptions. Do you have a coffee machine in your office that everyone comes by to use? Get rid of it. Do you leave your office door open all day long, extending a welcome to anyone who wants to intrude? Establish a closed door policy for at least two hours of the day. This forces visitors to ask your secretary if you are in, at which point she can tell them how busy you are right now.

Just as you discuss several matters in one phone call, you can cover many topics in one conversation, thus avoiding further interruptions. I call this the "Stand Up Meeting." If you pass Joe Smith in the hall, and you pause to say hello, be sure to discuss something important, too. Cover a project that Joe's involved in which is also one of your priorities. Get information, give information — do anything worthwhile during this moment in the hallway. In this manner you can eliminate more interruptions in the future.

One final trick for avoiding phone calls and visits: Start

assigning work to interruptors. When they call and waste your time, give them a little extra something to do. It's best if this assignment relates to your goals and priorities. Once you start delegating by interruption, you'll be amazed how quickly they stop bothering you.

What about meetings? Is there any way to avoid them? The secret to avoiding meetings is honesty. And it's the only tactic that works. If you truly have a project to do which is more important than a scheduled meeting, be honest about it. Your associates and co-workers are supposedly interested in the well-being of the company. If they understand that you can contribute more to the company by skipping the meeting than by attending, they should let you go without recriminations. But be cautious! If you do this too often, or without real need, you may soon be out of a job.

Let's pause and review your progress. What have you accomplished through this interruption management program?

1.   You know who is interrupting you.
2.   You know when the interruptions occur.
3.   You have created criteria for classifying important and important interruptions.
4.   You form objectives: you know how much time you waste with interruptions, and how much of that time you'd like to save.
5.   You have a list of constant interruptors. Your secretary holds all calls from these people, except emergencies.
6.   You have begun to recognize the personal problems that cause interruptions.
7.   You have established a Quiet Hour.
8.   You've minimized employee interruptions through good legating and daily staff meetings.
9.   You have a V.I.P. list. Only these people get you directly during high priority work.
10. You are keeping important calls and visits brief.

11. You get more out of important calls and avoid future interruptions by handling two or three matters simultaneously.
12. You've minimized wasteful visits.

It's quite difficult to estimate how much time you are now saving. But if you save only one hour each day, that adds up to almost a full day every month, and more than two extra weeks in a single year. What could you do with two free weeks?

By way of a summary, let me make one more point about interruptions. When you're forced to stop important work for relatively trivial phone calls or visits, how do you feel? Probably a little angered, frustrated, and abused. Now you've lost time on the work you're trying to accomplish. As a result, the job will take longer and get done later. How does that make you feel? Guilty, inadequate, insecure.

Soon, the emotional problems interruptions produce are interruptions of their own. You stop and think about them. They bother you at work and at home. That little interruption has snowballed into an emotional strife.

Interruptions work as a cycle. External interruption to less work to internal interruption to less work still. It's a powerful system, one that plagues almost every businessman in this world.

You can break the cycle. Start small, stop those silly little calls and chats. The result that you gain — the time you save — will be substantial.

11

Getting Your Paperwork in Order

One of the best ways to reduce stress is to get organized.

— Robert I. Woolfolk
and Frank C. Richardson

I have a friend who works at an exceedingly messy desk. Papers, files, and books are piled everywhere while he's on the job. In fact, he generates so much clutter that he has had to have a special desk created for him. It is eight feet long, has eighteen drawers, and still, from nine to five, you can rarely see the top of it for all the paperwork. And yet this fellow is one of the most effective managers I've ever known. Sometimes it seems he is single-handedly striving to solve the problem of America's declining productivity.

He has an original theory. "You're familiar with the laws of thermodynamics, John; physicists say that there is only a fixed amount of matter and energy in the universe. If there's order in one part of the universe, it can only be at the expense of chaos somewhere else. I've come to the same conclusion about order and chaos in my own life. If I spent my time worrying about keeping the top of my desk neat enough to pass a sergeant's inspection, it would only use up energy that could be better spent getting my work done and done well. The chaos on my desk is an indication of order elsewhere in my life — or so I like to think.''

A neat rationalization! But there may be an element of truth in it. Maintaining a clean desk is primarily an aesthetic consideration. The important thing is not to keep your working spaces as barren and clean as the pictures you see in interior decorators' magazines. Rather, the key issue is to make sure that every paper that lands on your desk is going somewhere. Problems arise when old business gets hopelessly mixed up with new business, creating a traffic jam on your desk and interfering with your moment to moment functioning. The following questions are the acid test of your workspace organization:

1. Do you waste more than ten minutes a day looking for important papers?
2. At any time during the past month, have you come across a paper in or on your desk that you had completely forgotten about?
3. Do you ever get the urge to sweep everything on top of your desk into a wastebasket?
4. Are there times when you feel that your methods for handling paperwork are just plain inadequate?

If you answered yes to any of these questions, then your ''input-output'' arrangements need rethinking.

Clare Booth Luce has a reputation for being an extraordinarily productive manager. And it has been said that the secret of her success was that she never handled a piece of paper more than once. Whether that was strictly true, I do not know. But the principle is basically sound. Papers come to your desk for action. When you respond with inaction or procrastination, things begin to pile up and you fall behind.

Essentially, there are four kinds of action you can take, whether dealing with paperwork in the office or at home:

1. You can throw it away.

2. You can file the paper for future reference.
3. You can pass it along to someone else (your secretary, your boss, your assistant, your spouse) for action.
4. Or, you can act on it yourself.

As you might have recognized, these four actions correspond almost perfectly with the Four D's — drop, delay, delegate, or do. Your goal should be to make a prompt decision as to which of these four resources is appropriate to each and every item that comes across your desk. But before we go further into this decision-making process, let's back up a step and see how you can reduce the amount of paperwork you have to cope with in the first place.

Your secretary can help by screening out all letters and papers that you don't really need to see. Some people have an irresistible urge to see every piece of mail that comes in with their names on it. The sooner you extinguish this desire the better. Your secretary is perfectly capable of deciding what's junk and what's not. He or she can also handle routine acknowledgments and filing without your direction. If your secretary can't perform these tasks, you need a more capable assistant. A secretary can and should be more than a typist and message-taker.

Next, where possible, you can discourage the needless production of memos in your office. Instead of churning out a separate memo, on a separate piece of paper, for each order of business, encourage your workers to compose summaries, bringing together a series of important communications on a single sheet. General messages of interest to many people in your office can be placed on a bulletin board, thus saving on paper, duplication, and effort.

You can probably think of other ways to reduce the flow of paper in your office. You could, for instance, schedule a five-minute staff meeting to communicate general messages rather than putting everything on a memo. You could acknowledge receipt of papers and respond by scrawling an informal note across the top and returning the communication (keeping a copy when necessary) rather than composing a full-fledged letter. You can restrict the processing of incoming papers, with the exception of truly urgent messages, to certain times of the day; that way you won't be continually interrupted by trivial memos.

At the same time that you're doing everything you can to minimize unnecessary paperwork, you should also be developing a series of categories to facilitate quick processing of the papers you do receive. Three general categories should suffice: "for immediate attention"; "work in progress"; and "reserve materials." The lattermost should be kicked back to your secretary and kept under her control. They are either earmarked for action a long time off or are to be kept for reference only. If some future action is required, you might indicate when this action is to occur on top of the paper. Have your secretary routinely make a note on her calendar to remind you in advance when you must act on "reserve materials."

The middle category of "work in progress" is trickier. What I have in mind here is papers that you will probably need to handle within the day or at most within the week. These papers should be filed in a location where you can gain immediate access to them without searching.

The "immediate attention" category should not be filed at all, at least not yet. They should remain on your desk, no more than an arm's length away, until you have initiated action on them. Now it may not be possible to follow in the footsteps of Clare Booth Luce and handle every paper only once. But the important point is this:

EVERY TIME YOU TOUCH A PAPER, YOU SHOULD BRING THE TASK IT REPRESENTS ONE STEP CLOSER TO COMPLETION.

Plan your next move. Schedule it if necessary. Make a call.

Dictate a letter. Delegate the job. Do something — anything — to start the ball rolling. In sports, in politics, in every aspect of achievement, momentum is essential. You should be making forward progress on every project that engages your attention. When you pick a paper up, read it, put it down again, then do nothing about it, you have squandered your time. You have been reduced to a "paper shuffler." If you don't act at once, inevitably you will have to read the paper all over again at a later date to refresh your memory. In the long run, you'll find it far, far better to take a first step now, no matter how small a step it is, than to do nothing at all.

Now that you have a system in mind, I recommend that you go through your desk tomorrow and begin to apply it. Ask yourself the following questions:

> Will I need this paper in the upcoming week? If not, relocate it. If yes, classify it for "immediate attention" or as "work in progress."

> Do I have a system for calling to my attention papers and projects that are now "on reserve" but will at some point be of immediate concern? If not, review the scheduling recommendations presented in Chapter Eight.

> Do I have all the supplies I need (pencils, scissors, dictionary, etc.) to handle my everyday tasks without interruption? If not, acquire them immediately.

Organizing your desk is merely the beginning of the course. When you see how much easier it makes your life, you will want to carry this campaign on to your personal finances and your home life. The benefits are far ranging. When you know where things are and have a plan for getting things done, it makes for a much more relaxed, easy-going existence.

This self-quiz will give you a chance to evaluate your present state of organization and may point to ways you can run a tighter ship.

DO YOU HAVE?

Yes _____ No _____   1. A set of extra keys for auto, home, and possessions located in a safe place?

Yes _____ No _____   2. An updated list of credit card numbers and places to call if they are lost or stolen?

Yes _____ No _____   3. Your will and other important documents put away in a safe place — a place your executor knows about?

Yes _____ No _____   4. A file containing the warranties and instructions for all your major appliances and possessions?

Yes _____ No _____   5. A list of all valuables that could be stolen, including their serial numbers stored in a safe place?

Yes _____ No _____   6. A current inventory of all household possessions for insurance purposes?

Yes _____ No _____   7. A current calendar or datebook noting all key personal dates, birthdays, anniversaries, social events?

Yes _____ No _____   8. A current financial plan showing major payment due dates (insurance, etc.) and dates when income (dividends, etc.) is scheduled to arrive?

Yes _____ No _____   9. Items in your car for emergencies — such as flashlight, jumper cables, wrench, screwdriver?

Yes _____ No _____   10. A current estate plan and instructions that could be followed by your survivors in case of your premature departure?

If you can honestly answer "yes" to nine or ten of the pre-
ceding questions, you are quite well organized. Seven or eight
yeses is still a respectable score. But six or fewer yeses is a clear
indication that you have some shaping up to do.

12

Speed Learning

Knowledge is of two kinds: we know a subject ourselves, or we know where we can find information about it.

—Samuel Johnson

When you're a young man seeking employment, it is often who you know that counts. But once established in business, no matter what the nature of it may be — it is what you know that truly matters. Certainly you know how to do your job. But do you know how others are handling the same business? Do you know what the top people in your field are thinking, doing, investigating? Are you educating yourself for tomorrow? Do you know exactly how your boss operates so you'll be ready to step into his shoes?

In any human activity — especially business — knowledge is essential. Without information and communication, you simply cannot function. And if you want to get ahead in business, you must constantly be developing, learning more, understanding more about your field of interest.

Today more than ever, the man who gets ahead in corporate America is the man who has educated himself. He's the one who always has a finger on current trends in industry . . . new technical developments, and theories . . . what the competition is doing . . . what the experts predict for the future. The successful businessman is the one who can make information his tool.

There is also a tremendous need for information outside the corporate structure. Without up-to-date facts and figures, a small businessman can lose his shirt. Your personal finances can be wasted or lost if you don't know what you're buying or what you're investing in. Even your health is in jeopardy without accurate knowledge of nutrition and disease.

Make no mistake: information is success. The people who learn make the right moves, get the promotions, buy the right stocks. The others — the people who do not learn — fall behind, a little further every day.

Every day of your life, you communicate — you exchange information — but what do you learn? How do you assimilate the information into yourself, promoting growth and development? Most often, people either forget what they have been exposed to or ignore the information altogether. The opportunity to learn and grow is always present, and yet most businessmen do not take advantage of it.

Does this sound like you: You're a bad reader. You read very slowly, usually finding yourself bored or confused after a few minutes. After reading something, you tend to forget what it said. You read things that catch your eye, like advertisements, and skip articles and books that relate to your work or personal interests.

You're a bad communicator. When talking, you tend to be long-winded, indirect, and boring. When listening, you lose concentration, fail to notice the important points mentioned, and forget what people have said. In writing, you join words together that make no sense, hide the important facts, and take too long getting to the point.

The Hour Power "Speed Learning" program divides the topic of learning into two categories: study and communication. Study is the pursuit of valuable knowledge and information. It is developing yourself, expanding your boundaries, with the objective purpose of attaining your goals. Communication is the give and take of information. It occurs in speech, writing and listening.

The Hour Power Program will give you the guidelines for becoming a better learner. It will help you study more often and more efficiently. And it will help you overcome the communications problems that destroy efficiency and turn success into failures.

After admitting that you are a bad reader, speaker, listener, and writer, it's time to find out why.

Let's consider your reading habits. Why are they so poor? Why do you find it almost impossible to sit down and read a book from cover to cover? I believe it is because of the attitudes and habits you have developed in life.

Most of us made our first attempts at structured learning in school. And the experiences gained here have made us all bad learners. The school child quickly learns one thing very well: school is not fun. Homework is not fun. This child has made a very accurate deduction. School and study were never intended to be fun. They were created for a purpose. Just as we work to earn money, we study to learn. The idea is that we will in some way benefit from what we discover.

This is where our bad habits come from. In school, we could never quite see the importance of all the studying. Who cares about Math? Who wants to read Milton? Because the work and its long-term rewards never seemed to meet, we formed a distinct impression that reading, studying and remembering were just meaningless tasks given to us, almost as a punishment.

When you attempt to read work-related materials, you probably still feel like a child doing homework. You approach the task as a burden, something you would never do if you didn't have to. Then you fall into the same habits that you had in grammar school. You avoid reading as long as possible. Once you begin, you allow your mind to wander. After reading a few pages, you suddenly discover that you haven't been paying attention.

Just like the school child, you are treating learning as a punishment. But the school child has an excuse being too young to realize how his studies will one day come in handy. You have no such excuse. You know that article on real estate will be valuable information for you, and still you don't read it. You have the bad reading habit so deeply engrained in your mind that you cannot break it even when you want to.

But what if you could break these habits, change these attitudes? What if you could double your reading rate while increasing comprehension? Would you like to digest the vital information from dozens of books and magazines every week? What if you could communicate more quickly, more clearly, listen accurately, get every detail and nuance of intonation? You'd be a better businessman, a better homemaker, a better provider. You'd be on top of things for a change, instead of years behind. You'd be more successful.

But how can you break the habits of a lifetime and begin to form new learning skills? As in every other phase of the Hour Power System, you can change your life through evaluation and planning: you form goals, decide on steps you want to take, changes you want to make . . . then you form a positive program that will guide you to those goals. Here's the step by step process. First you must find out what you are doing now, determine exactly what is holding you back, and then correct the situation.

Since learning is a two-part matter, let's attack it one part at a time. First, study.

In the early sixties, after years of consistent growth and expansion, modern business began to realize that it was barely keeping up with itself. The tremendous amount of information, growing every day, was not being communicated within the company. Corporations realized that the creation and development of effective executives depended on learning. From training programs to high-level management seminars, business began to encourage its employees to learn — about new developments, changing methods, and expectations for the future.

Many corporations developed elaborate technologies for educating their executives. Following the example of liberal school systems, they emphasized audio-visual materials and electronic communication. Slide shows, training films, video programs, special testing equipment — hundreds of thousands of dollars were spent on learning technology.

But then, after these elaborate systems had been in service for several years, both the schools and the corporations discovered the the programs were not producing the desired results. After lots of wasted time and money, little Johnny still couldn't read, and big Johnny still didn't get his promotion.

So the educators and corporations began searching for a new method of learning . . . something that would produce better results at a lower expense. Could there be some other way for an individual to find information, share the wisdom of others, and gain experience by studying the experiences of other people?

They arrived at the amazing source of learning they had searched for: reading. Teachers realized that if you want a child to read, you must teach him to read. Watching a slide show or film will not teach anyone how to read.

Corporations made the same discovery. They found that by selecting the right materials and obliging executives to read them, they could develop more intelligent, more educated employees. The system was easy to organize, very low in cost, and very high in results.

But what about you, the bad reader? How can you hope to keep up with your business, much less excel, if you cannot keep up with current knowledge and information?

There are many reasons why corporations encourage their employees to study. The major purpose is training. Large companies will hire college graduates and pay them handsome salaries for a full year without requiring them to work or produce. All they have to do is study and learn the business. Corporations also encourage their top people to read during work time in the hope that they will find out about the newest trends and developments going on in their field. At other times, employees are encouraged to learn how to overcome knowledge deficiencies. So many companies find themselves with underqualified employees that this kind of after-the-fact training is necessary. The final reason for corporate learning is preparation for new responsibilities. In order to form a pool of promotable, upward mobile executives, companies demand reading, learning, and study.

Among these reasons, which relate to you? Do you want to train yourself? Find new ideas? Catch up on things you should know, but don't? Prepare yourself for new, exciting tasks?

To find the answer, you must return to your four major goals in life. For the sake of demonstration, I'll create some average goals that may be a lot like your own.

First, you want to succeed in your career. Second, you would like to make some smart investments and manage your money well. Third, you want to develop certain personal interests which give you a sense of fulfillment and make you a more interesting person. And finally, you want to be a good spouse and parent.

Since we are primarily concerned with business reading now, I'll assign your first goal — career — the highest priority. If your most important desire in life is therefore to succeed in work, how can reading help you attain this goal?

Do you want to train yourself for a particular career? Do you want to remain abreast of the most current developments in your field? Are you concerned that you may be under-qualified for your present position and wish to improve your knowledge and skill? Or do you want to prepare for an anticipated promotion or new responsibility?

The choice is completely yours. But you needn't feel pressured to limit your reading too much. Many of these reading purposes overlap to a great degree. But by analyzing your goal and these four topics of study in business, you will be able to form a list of reading matter you can benefit from.

On a blank piece of paper, list all the material you'd like to be reading. This might include trade papers and magazines in your industry, special business magazines and papers, newspapers, periodicals, and even current books on business and finance. Again, the choice is very personal and subjective. Only you can make it. Now, arrange some time tomorrow to buy or borrow every one of these materials. You are going to read every one of them.

The next step is to analyze what you are reading now, when and why you are reading these things, and exactly how you are going to change. I call it an "Objective Reading Analysis."

Starting from a chart detailing exactly what you read now, list the title and nature of the subject matter, the time you began reading and the time you stopped, and why you wanted to read this in the first place.

Your first entry should look like this:

	Title	Nature	Start/Stop	Purpose
1.	HOUR POWER	time management program	6:30	To use my time better

From this point on, continue to list everything you read.

If you read fairly often, it may only take a few hours to pin-point your bad reading habits. For others, a few days of analysis may be necessary.

Once you have about two dozen entries on your chart, it's time to evaluate. If you've been honest, you've listed every let-ter, advertisement, headline, and container label you've read.

How much of what you've been reading relates to your goals? What's the ratio of important business reading to useless, wasteful study? In my research, I've discovered that most people devote more than 90 percent of their reading time and effort to material that in no way relates to any of their goals.

Look at all that wasted time! Make a promise to yourself: from this moment on you will use this same amount of reading time — not a minute more — for important learning. You will not spend any more time on reading, but you will begin to gain something more from the time you spend.

Even if you spent less than one hour each day reading, you are now going to read all the materials you listed earlier (which you have now acquired) — and do it within a few short hours!

But how? Your list probably contains four magazines, a few newspapers, and even a book or two. How can you possibly read this much in a few hours? By simply learning how to read correctly. You know from your own bad reading habits that you now read incorrectly. It's time to change this habit and replace it with a dynamic new study skill.

You've probably heard about speed reading. There are lots of organizations that will teach you speed reading with lots of different techniques. I have no intention of disparaging these methods, and in fact if you have the time and money, I suggest you investigate one of these programs yourself. But for now, let's talk about one simple step that can increase your reading speed tremendously without special courses or difficult study tricks. It's called "Selective Reading."

Stop and consider how you read right now. You pick up a book, flip to the first chapter, and start reading the first sentence. You continue reading every word in the book until you either finish or give up or fall asleep. How many of these sentences have anything to do with your goals? How much necessary information are you taking in and then forgetting? In this flood of words and phrases, have you overlooked something that was truly important to you?

This kind of reading reflects two forms of procrastination: perfectionism and muddling. First, you feel you must begin reading at the beginning and work your way carefully toward the end. For some reason you may not even be aware of, this appeals to your sense of order and neatness. It's perfectionism, and it's a waste of time and effort.

Secondly, as you read you dawdle and fumble, losing your place, stopping to daydream. If a section doesn't seem to make sense, you don't skip it and move on. You read it twice! And after the second reading, it still doesn't mean much to you.

The alternative to this kind of reading is Selective Reading. A more common term for this is "skimming." It starts when you first pick up the book, magazine or newspaper. Ask yourself, "Why am I reading this?" Remember your goals and how this reading matter relates to them. Psych yourself up for reading — take it on like a battle and decide right now that you are going to be victorious.

Now you can open the book. The first thing to do is to go directly to the chapter listing, or table of contents. Read the title of each chapter, any descriptions of what that chapter contains, and try to decide what that section has to offer you. In this way, you will isolate the chapters that relate to your goals, and skip the sections that do not.

Now, open the book to the chapter that relates to you, but

don't start reading the first sentence. Instead, do the exact opposite. Read the last paragraph of the chapter first. This will show you exactly where you are going. This last paragraph is your goal. It will help you to understand what the chapter has to offer, what you should be looking for, and what you may discover.

Now go back to the first page and remind yourself of the chapter title and what you are looking for here. Then flip slowly through the pages, glancing at each of them briefly. Look for subheadings, underlined phrases, italicized words, and capitalized nouns.

As you flip through, you will see the patterns of this chapter. You will recognize an idea being developed, analyzed, and annotated. By the time you reach the end, you will know exactly how the writer worked his way from the chapter title to that last paragraph you read. Now you can go back and begin reading.

Read as quickly as possible. Once you have the basic idea of any sentence, skip on to the next one. If a paragraph starts to ramble, or simply seems to get bogged down, skip it and begin the next one. When something seems important, pause and give it enough time for proper comprehension.

Feel free to jump ahead whenever you like. When you jump, see if you can still follow what's being discussed. You may find that you have skipped something essential, in which case you should go back. But in most cases, you will skip several paragraphs without missing a thing, and save lots of time as a bonus.

When you reach the end of the chapter, see if you understand what you have read. In your mind (or better still, on paper), try to form a few sentences that sum up the material you have read. If you have skimmed effectively, you will be able to capsulize the many pages of words in just a few phrases.

Now, return to the beginning again and give the chapter one

more fast skim. The purpose of this is to remind yourself of exactly what you have just read. After skimming the chapter twice and fast reading it once, the information it contains should be yours forever.

This style of reading is virtually unchanged for magazines. Begin with the table of contents. As obvious as this seems, most people simply don't do it. In another study I made, more than 95 percent of the people I tested never even glanced at the table of contents in magazines. They simply open it and start flipping through — often from back to front!

Naturally, you should read only the articles that relate to your goals, and you will follow the same steps as above: Read the last paragraph first, skim it quickly, read it fast and skip ahead, then skim it once again.

There is one extra trick that helps when reading magazines: always skip the first paragraph of each article. I've discovered that in the majority of magazine articles, the first paragraph tells absolutely nothing.

When reading newspapers, the technique is a little different. This is because newspapers are designed to accommodate speed reading. Essentially, the headline and first paragraph tell the whole story. News writers are trained to express the entire story in their very first sentence! If only everything was written this way!

The better newspapers contain detailed tables of contents that will tell you the nature of the major articles inside. Use such a table of contents to select what you will read.

Other papers, like *The New York Times,* have a special section in which all the major news of the day is told within a few dozen sentences. If your paper contains such a "news-at-a-glance" section, read it first and then investigate only the stories that interest you.

When reading newspapers articles, read the headline first and then the first paragraph. Do not read any further unless the article is of particular interest to you.

If you begin using these techniques tonight, you will effectively double or even triple your reading speed immediately.

"But this isn't really reading," you may think. "I'm just skipping around!" Are you? What is the point of reading? Isn't it to find information that is important to you? Isn't that exactly what you have done?

You may feel this kind of reading is cheating, but only because of bad habits you picked up long ago, probably in grammar school. Forget about being perfect. Start being effective.

Now that you are reading selectively, you can also start practicing another speed-reading technique: getting someone else to do it.

Remember the four D's? Why not delegate reading? If you've followed the Hour Power Program so far, you already have your secretary pre-reading your mail. Why not let her do this with other reading materials? She can read it when she has nothing else to do, then condense it for you or simply highlight the important passages. For the sake of your department's efficiency and productivity, I urge you to get your employees and assistants to start reading more. First, share the ideas you've gotten here with them. Let them read this book, or hand out copies of these pages.

But how can you make someone else read if they don't want to? Well, you can make it mandatory. You can run your reading program just like a school. Assign the reading, give a deadline, and have them write reports. It's not much fun, but it usually works.

But there's another method: make them want to read.

You can give incentives to your employees who read and report interesting information to you. You can hold meetings in which your staff discusses interesting reading they've done lately. You can even let them schedule work hours for learning, or pay them for hours spent reading at home.

It might seem wasteful at first, but in the long run a knowledgeable staff will reflect well on you and bring you that much closer to attaining your goals.

And why not share these ideas with your school-age children? Or even with your friends and relatives? Learning is a life-long process. No matter what you do, or how old you may be, you have something to gain from reading correctly.

Now, what about the other communications skills that can produce learning? Namely speaking, listening and writing? If you're like more people, you have the same problems here as in your reading. You waste words, forget things, obscure essential points, ramble, and get bored. You are constantly sending and receiving important information, and yet you are not gleaning any real knowledge from your efforts.

The solution is essentially the same for communicating as for reading: be selective. Skim over the meaningless and linger on the important.

When speaking, get directly to the point. Don't meander around what you have to say, spinning anecdotes and giving unimportant background information. If you want to tell someone a vital shipment has arrived, don't start off by saying "You know, I was just on the telephone with Jack. Say, did you know his wife just had a baby?" Instead, simply say: "Hello. Jack says the shipment has arrived." Skip the little fine points that make nice dinner conversation. This is work, not pleasure, so get to the point and get it over with.

The same is true for your writing. I know so many people who say, "I can't write a decent letter." The problem with these individuals is not their writing abilities, but rather their conception of what makes a good letter. Just as in conversation, the best letter will say simply: "Dear Ed: Jack says the shipment has arrived.'' That's it. No wasted words. No flowery sentences. Straight to the point and goodbye.

When possible in writing use a shorthand approach. For example just after Jack called and told you about the arrival of that shipment, you could have made a notation that looked like this: Jack: "Shipment In". Think of it like a newspaper headline, telling the whole story in three or four words. This note can be passed along to your secretary with two or three bits of explanation and she will create a fine letter from it.

Perhaps the finest model of speed writing is the telegram. Think of how quickly it expresses an idea: "Arrived, 10:30. Feel fine. Will call tonight." You see, when we have to pay for words, we quickly find ways to eliminate them.

Why not do this all the time? Every time you write something, imagine you are paying for extra words. Cut out any words that don't say something concrete. And don't worry about grammar! This isn't an English test, it's a business memo (perfectionism, again!).

For the sake of memory, keep a copy of all your important business writing. But be careful! Drop all paperwork that isn't really important in the wastebasket! Keeping copies of unimportant paperwork is a major time waster.

So far, you have discovered how to read, speak and write effectively. But what about listening? How can you capture all the useful information that people bring to you in conversation and put it to use?

Again, the key is to be selective. We've all had the bad luck of being stuck with a boring conversationalist at a party. You can spot him after the first few sentences. You know almost instantly that this person has nothing to say of any value. Naturally, you let this bore's pearls of wisdom float in one ear and out the other. You wouldn't waste time concentrating and retaining pointless words. If you can use these same methods of ignoring the unimportant, and add to it a technique of isolating the essential, you can begin to learn from conversation — and again take a step toward your goals.

To uncover the wasteful points in other people's speaking, apply the techniques of effective speaking in reverse. You already learned not to waste your words on unimportant background and scene setting. So you can now look for these same time wasters in other people. When you sense someone is wasting time with this kind of useless talk, don't pay any attention. When you know they have finally come to the point, listen carefully and remember what is said. If necessary, take notes on the important information covered. Or use association techniques to help you remember. This is another popular and well-publicized method, utilizing rhymes, symbols, or numerals to help you recall important information. The concept is a simple one: by associating a vital piece of information with a common and memorable symbol, you can help yourself recall the information later.

Besides ignoring wasted words and concentrating on the important points, there are many easy ways to direct other people's speech and thereby improve your listening abilities. Directing conversation is something you already do all the time but probably not when it can be of the most value. For example, when talking with a friend you don't hesitate to change subjects or say, "listen, tell me about this . . ." But when talking with clients and superiors, you may find it hard to lead the conversation. You probably tend to listen to whatever is said and hope for the best.

But through tactful persuasion, you can get anyone to come to the point without seeming pushy or forward. The secret is to gently lead their train cf thought in the direction you want. Let's say someone is wasting words describing the background or circumstances that lead to the information you need to know. Suppose they are telling you about a new contract, and first they are setting the scene with lots of detail and dialogue.

You can simply cut in at a given point, after paying close attention to what they've been saying, and ask, "Is that when you signed the contract?" or something of that nature. Chances are, you will be able to get the procrastinating communicator to leap ahead to the important facts and skip the trivia.

One final quip about effective listening: If the conversation is vital, have it in privacy. Avoid interruptions and distractions at all costs when communicating truly substantial information. For the best results, take this kind of conversation inside your office, with the door closed, and your phone calls on hold.

It may seem unbelievable, but of all the important information we hear, say, and write every day, most of us retain only a tiny percentage. The rest is wasted and forgotten. And if you add to this all the useful literature you aren't reading — or, still worse, that you are reading and not recalling — you can honestly say that you are ignoring almost all the important information that would help you had you learned it instead of overlooking it.

What could you do with this information? One thing only: attain your life's goals. Are you willing to do a little studying in order to have what you most desire?

Through practicing the techniques outlined in this chapter, anyone — from a retired executive of 66 to a small child of 5 just starting school — can learn more, remember more and save time formerly spent reading and communicating improperly.

Don't forget: reading and communicating are the paths to learning. And learning is the way to success.

13

Tips For Trips

Travel, in the younger sort, is a part of education; in the elder, a part of experience.

— Francis Bacon

Getting around is a lot easier than it used to be. Just a few hundred years ago, a 50-mile journey could take up to two days. Today, some people commute to work further than this.

But if traveling has gotten easier, it's also gotten a lot more complex. We have periodic gas shortages that make car travel almost impossible. Events like the DC-10 grounding make travel a matter of balanced risks. Flights are delayed or cancelled. Baggage is misplaced or stolen. Room reservations are now often harder to get than at any other point in our history.

If you're trying to get from here to there quickly, the odds are stacked up against you. And whatever tricks and secrets you can acquire about traveling easier must come from painful, aggravating experience.

In my travels as a time management lecturer, I've had lots of bad experiences. But through experience, I have been able to evaluate the travel problem, and I have come upon several tips that will make your travel more efficient, productive, and pleasant.

Of course, the vast majority of your travel time is spent getting to and from work. There are really only two ways to improve this situation. Either find a better, faster route or mode of transportation. Or else make your commutation a "two-for-one" arrangement. On a bus or train, you can read or do business. In a car, you can use a cassette deck to dictate letters or play tapes that will educate you or prepare you for today's business.

There are, however, a large number of things you can do to make business trips and vacations more successful. When you're going somewhere to enjoy your only free weeks of the year, you want as few hassles as possible. The tips in this chapter should help every vacationer enjoy himself a little more.

But primarily, I want to talk about business trips. Recent surveys indicate that at least 70% of all executives take a minimum of one business related trip each year. How can you make these work-vacations more time and cost efficient?

The first step is to evaluate the importance of any trip. Do you really need to go? Could someone else go in your place? How long do you really have to stay? Could you avoid the trip by using the telephone or conducting your business by mail? Any trip you can skip is an easy journey.

If you must go, your first destination should be the office of a good travel agent. If you are reserving your own flight tickets, finding your own hotel accommodations, or even having your secretary take care of it, you are wasting time and money. A travel agent will make all these arrangements — probably with better results — at no charge or for a few dollars at the most. The experienced travel agent is a trained expert, and his or her valuable talents are at your service free of charge. Why not take advantage of them?

To locate a good travel agent, I suggest you rely on word of mouth. But don't take the advice of someone who refers to trips he or she took years ago. The travel picture has changed so quickly and so thoroughly that only recent information is of any value. Get someone who travels often to recommend an agent they trust.

It is wise to make use of your agent's knowledge by accepting all his or her advice, as long as it doesn't run completely contrary to your plans. For example, he may suggest the trains instead of airlines for your particular destination, or he may recommend one airline over another. Unless you know more than the agent, follow his advice.

Another advantage of travel agents is that they tend to carry more clout than do individual travelers. They deal with airlines and hotels every day and are probably well known by the people they do business with. They can find the best arrangement at the best prices. Studies show that American business spends more than $7 billion every year through travel agents. There must be a good reason.

The next things to do before you travel, and preferably in cooperation with your travel agent, is to analyze the nature of your journey and evaluate your travel goals, for they will determine your arrangements. Consider what kind of business you will be doing and who you will be meeting with. Then decide what kind of accommodation would be most appropriate. If prestige is essential, you may want to go first class all the way. But if the trip is routine, an inexpensive motel near the airport might be just fine. For similar reasons, you might elect to rent a car or simply to take cabs and buses. How long you stay at your destination may also be determined by the importance of the trip. For a simple contract signing, a few hours may do. But if you're going to establish a rapport with a new client, you may want to stay for several days. Whatever your arrangements may be, always prepare alternatives.

Now it's time to form a checklist for your trip. This should include your flight number and departure time, your proposed arrival time, the address and phone number of your hotel, and specific details on each appointment and activity you anticipate. Your checklist, if properly designed, should include all vital data as well as a complete schedule of how you will spend your time.

Carry this checklist with you at all times, and date it when necessary. Be sure to write down any new numbers, addresses, times, and dates. Wasting mental energy on trying to remember details is pointless. Write them down where you can find them, and you're free to forget about them until they're needed.

Your checklist should also include a section in which you can list all the items you should be taking with you— from clothing to business materials and paperwork. Start building the list immediately and add to it or delete items as your trip grows closer and closer. Through this kind of writing and re-evaluating, you can avoid dragging along lots of necessary items. I'll have more on this later.

The next step in getting ready for your trip is probably the most essential. You must prepare yourself for failures. Remember Murphy's law? "If something can go wrong, it will. And at the least convenient time." This humorous constant is always evident in traveling. From traffic jams on the highway to stacked jets over the runways, traveling is fraught with breakdowns and failures.

The only way to get through the barriers and reach your destination is to have contingency plans ready when emergencies occur. Generally, it is wise to plan everything twice. Have two ways to get to the airport, two possible flights you can take should one be cancelled, two hotel rooms reserved, two ways to get from the airport to your hotel. Whatever you are doing, prepare an alternative plan. This way, when things go wrong, you can use your alternate plan instead of simply accepting what is available — or getting nowhere.

The chances of arriving anywhere on time grow increasingly bleak these days. You should be prepared for delays and have something with you to pass what would be wasted hours. Bring a little extra work or one extra book. While you might never get to this additional material, it could prove useful if your travel time is suddenly doubled due to delay.

Also be prepared for time changes when you travel. Crossing time zones leaves many people in a minor haze called "jet lag". If you've done much business traveling across time zones, you know this can be a problem, expecially when your disorientation is increased by a few drinks in flight. If you're aware of the time changes you will experience, you can prepare yourself for them by adjusting your sleeping schedule a few days before your trip. In this way, you will be more prepared for the new time schedule when you arrive at your destination.

Before you travel, you must be aware of the environmental changes your new location will create. Be sure you know what the weather is like where you are going. Obviously, if you're going to Miami from Boston in December, you should not bring your snow shoes. And yet, it might be wise to bring along a sweater. The only way to be sure is to check recent weather conditions in your destination. Again, get your travel agent's advice.

One of the best things you can do to avoid wasting travel time and money is to travel light. The fewer items you bring along, the less time you will spend dropping off luggage, collecting it again, going through customs checks, loading and unloading cabs or buses. The lighter you travel, the better off your are. If at all possible, I recommend you take only what you can carry on board the plane or the train. If you manage to do this you not only eliminate the wait and waste of baggage claim lines, but you also dramatically reduce the chance of theft and damage to your property. The carry-on bag is right there with you. You can get it quickly, and you can be sure of its safety.

If you can't get away with so little luggage, do your best to bring only as many bags as you can carry yourself. When you drag along more luggage than you can get under your own arms, you are asking for delays and problems. Unless someone will be waiting for you at your destination, you will have to find a porter to help you carry your bags. You'll have to pay him, too. The same holds true for cabdrivers and bellhops. So, bring as little as possible and you'll save time and money.

Always be sure to carry business or reading materials. You will be in transit for several hours, and you can get lots of work done in this time. There are few places in this world that are as interruption-free as the inside of an airplane. This provides the perfect setting for business reading, light paper work, or even reading for pleasure. Of course, if you're fond of having two or three drinks in a 90-minute flight, work might be out of the question. But if you can get some work done while traveling, you're getting two-for-one from your time.

When your bags are packed and your plans made, complete with alternatives and contingency arrangements, you are almost ready to leave home. Just before you go, call the airport and check on the status of your flight. If the flight is delayed or cancelled, ask about your alternative plan. You may want to take that second flight and avoid waiting. Also call the hotel where you will be staying to be sure they have your reservation. It is far better to uncover a foul-up before you leave than when you arrive in some distant city.

Whenever possible, try to schedule your flight so that you arrive at the airport at an off-peak hour and also so that you do not arrive at your destination during a rush hour. If you can do this, you will avoid aggravating traffic jams on both ends. If you must travel during peak times, leave yourself enough leeway to get where you are going in heavy traffic. In other words, don't plan to arrive at O'Hare at 5:15 and be in downtown Chicago at 5:25. It simply won't work out that way and you will be terribly late for your appointment. Be prepared for delays and you'll minimize the damage they do.

Whenever you visit a strange town, it is wise to leave extra time for almost everything. Since you have almost no way of predicting what delays or unique problems might arise in this new town, you should leave yourself plenty of time to deal with them. Get at early start when traveling around the city. and leave extra free time for correcting any unexpected problems that may arise.

The problems travelers face tend to come under specific categories. Here then are some ways to handle common problems and some ideas about saving time and money on trips:

WHAT TO CARRY ON TRIPS

When you're away from your office, your briefcase and jacket pockets must serve as your desk and filing cabinet. The most important object to carry is your checklist, which details all your plans and gives your complete schedule as well as phone numbers and addresses of importance. Never let this checklist out of your sight. It's also essential to carry a note pad and a pen, should you need to jot down notes and write messages. Bring lots of change to avoid waiting to break dollar bills. In fact, you should always try to carry smaller denominations of money while traveling. Anything that costs more than $50.00 should be put on your charge account.

Dedicate one pocket to receipts. If you want to write off this trip, or put it on your expense account, those receipts from dinners and cabs could prove very important.

Also be sure you have some personal credit cards, and bring along your telephone credit card if you have one. This is another nice time saver, especially if you run out of change.

Bring blank checks for expected expenses. And be sure to carry your personal identification and your driver's license should you want to rent a car.

A pocket atlas can also be invaluable when traveling, particularly if you find yourself driving on strange roads or getting an unrequested guided tour of the city from some unscrupulous cab driver. Look for atlases that give detailed maps of major cities, particularly those you travel to most often.

Finally, there is one vital piece of equipment every time saver should carry close to his heart: a watch. Without a watch, you're heading for trouble. Set your time with an official time service (check your phone book). Don't rely on passers by or cab drivers to give you the exact time of day.

GETTING THROUGH AIRPORTS

Airports are amazing places. From the outside, they look so calm and efficient. The buildings have lots of open space and present a quiet, relaxed atmosphere. Unfortunately, this is all window dressing. Getting through an airport can be downright impossible.

If you have managed to carry your luggage onto the plane, you have beaten the baggage claim dilemma. But if you must wait for your luggage, have something to do while you kill time. Read, work, whatever you like, but don't stand around looking bored watching for your bags to come down a ramp. In other words, be prepared to wait.

When selecting a flight, be aware that the last flights of the day are the ones that tend to get cancelled most often. If possible, pick a flight closer to peak hours. Avoid the rush hour if you can, but avoid the middle of the night, too.

The only way to beat the effects of jet lag is to alter your sleeping schedule a few days before your flight. Try to get on the schedule you are heading to, therefore minimizing the effects of time differences. You probably won't be able to take these preparatory steps for your trip back, but your condition upon return home is probably not as critical.

Some airlines are now offering an arrangent by which you check in once for two flights. This means you have your ticket verified only once for a round trip flight. Ask your travel agent about such plans, and if available, take advantage of them.

WHERE TO SIT ON THE PLANE

For most people, plane seats are not a matter of choice. But if you know ahead of time what your needs are, your travel agent may be able to arrange the exact seat you want in advance. Barring this, an early arrival at the airport will give you another chance to choose your seat, especially if you're among the first aboard the plane.

Where you sit should reflect what you plan to do during the flight. For example, if you want to daydream or sleep, find a window seat. If you are carrying on a bag or planning to work, take a seat on the aisle, it provides more room.

If you smoke heavily, especially a pipe or cigar, sit as far as possible from the no-smoking section and avoid complainers. If you want peace and quiet, sit as far from the engine as possible. Try to stay away from children if you plan to get some work done. If you're exceptionally hungry, take a seat near the stewardesses' work area so you'll be among the first served.

If you really need to get some work done on this flight, consider travelling in first class. This section gives you more arm and leg room and also tends to be quieter.

One special tip about airlines and preparing for failure: on every flight, the stewardess explains how to use the emergency equipment in the event of trouble. Naturally, no one pays any attention to her. I suggest you spend a few moments learning how to save your life in case danger arises. Keep Murphy's law in mind here and prepare yourself for possible crisis.

THE BEST WAY TO DEAL WITH HOTELS

When making hotel arrangements, it is essential to shop early and compare prices and services. Under no circumstances should you let advertising and famous names make your decisions. Call several hotels, or better still have your travel agent call them, and ask about prices and accommodations. Through comparison, you can find the best deal.

When you call the hotel to confirm your reservation, be sure to get the name of the person you speak to. This way, if any problem arises when you arrive at the hotel, you can say "Mr. Smith told me otherwise." This name dropping will lend power to your argument.

When you select your room, silence and privacy are often important qualities. You can use a little hotel-trade jargon to get your message across. In cities, ask for a room "high and inside." This means a room on an upper floor and not facing the street, thus minimizing traffic noise. At the airport, ask for a room "on the graveyard side." This is a pilot's term for the side of the hotel which faces away from the airport and is therefore quieter.

If you have any complaints about your accommodations, be sure to voice them loudly. You cannot expect to get quick effective action from big institutions like major hotels unless you raise a little hell. If you have problems, mention your company and refer to how much business you bring to this establishment. Let them know that if you are unhappy, no one from your company will ever come here again. Remind them of what they promised you and your intention to hold them to their offer.

If they offer you a new room, don't vacate the old one until you've inspected the new accommodations. It might be worse than where you are now. If you choose to move to a new room, be sure you can stay there for the duration of your trip and won't be shifted around anymore. If they give you a hard time about this, remind them of all the grief you have been through already and assure them you intend to take no more abuse.

Finally, if things are really unbearable, call your travel agent. Let him know you are disappointed with the arrangement he made and have him find you another hotel. If the new hotel seems preferable, get in a cab and make the move.

One special tip: for some reason, very few people ever consider the idea of bargaining with hotels. But believe me, it can be done. Usually, this technique of price bickering will not work if the hotel is crowded, but during the off season, you can often cut the price of accommodations considerably by just holding out. Of course, bargaining might get you nowhere, but you really have nothing to lose by trying.

SAVING MONEY WHEN TRAVELING

The cardinal rule for avoiding rip offs when traveling is NEVER TELL ANYONE YOU ARE NEW IN TOWN. Even if you go to Atlanta with a Brooklyn accent, tell people you come down this way all the time. The tourist who runs around telling salesmen and cabdrivers how little they know about this city are the easiest marks in the world. They wind up traveling five miles to get across a two-mile town. They pay the highest prices possible for second class goods. They have set themselves up to lose money. So under any circumstances, pretend you know something about where you are.

The second rule is IF YOU FEEL YOU ARE BEING RIPPED-OFF, SAY SO. There is no way to defend your rights and protect yourself unless you speak up. Be sure the people you suspect of thievery know you are ready and willing to take bold action against them. If you keep your complaints to yourself, you will never get results.

Whenever possible, travel off-season and you'll save a bundle. This rule applies to both business trips and vacations. When everyone in the world seems to be going to the same place, you can forget about finding bargains. Arrange your trips to occur at the least popular times and you can cut the cost of traveling in half.

Many airlines, hotels, restaurants and other places offer special deals to senior citizens, children, and businessmen. Unfortunately, they have a tendency to keep these special offers a well-guarded secret. Always ask if you are eligible for special rates or discounts, no matter where you go. You'll be amazed how many money-saving breaks are waiting for you to ask for them.

For corporations, there are several alternatives that might be more cost-efficient than commercial travel. Many large companies have purchased private jets and find that the time savings and convenience make the investment a bargain.

New technologies have provided other alternatives to travel for corporate executives. Conference calls, in which several people in many locations can all be on the same phone line, can be an excellent answer. You can do business with clients and associates in several cities without leaving your office. These calls are not inexpensive, of course, but they are considerably cheaper than business trips.

Some companies have purchased elaborate video tape equipment and now send recorded presentations on trips instead of businessmen. For some situations, this could be just perfect, although the personal quality that comes from face to face contact is lost. Consider the viability of such a system in your business and make your decision appropriately.

Another strange new development is what might be called rent-an-office. Some airports have office spaces, complete with secretaries, which traveling businessmen can rent on an hourly or daily basis. If you get stuck in an airport for any extended period of time, renting an office and secretary could be a great idea.

One final Big Tip to travelers: be prepared to wait. I cannot say this enough. Delays are inevitable. Have detailed, effective contingency plans for travel and accommodations. Bring extra work material and reading for unanticipated or extended delays. Leave a copy of your schedule with your secretary in case you lose yours. In other words, be prepared for the absolute worst to happen. It very well might.

Travel is a fact of modern life. A few hundred years ago, people seldom journeyed beyond their own towns and villages. The man who had made the long trek from country to city or who had been to the state capital was something of a celebrity. But today, almost everyone travels some distance to work, and the majority of Americans have traveled by plane. We are now a mobile people.

In the years to come, travel will probably grow more difficult rather than more simple. Planes, trains, and highways will be more crowded. Fuel shortages will force prices up and create fewer airline flights. Human error will continue to be a problem, and computer malfunctions will probably become even more common with growing work loads.

You can't expect travel to be easy. Getting from one place to another is work, and it takes effort. But consider for a moment what travel would be like without engines and planes and cars. How would you like to have to walk to your next convention?

There is only one way to make traveling easier and more pleasant: be prepared, get organized, and hold your temper. Don't allow yourself to become frustrated over delays and obstacles, they are inevitable. You can't escape them completely.

But you can diminish the headaches of getting around by anticipating trouble, and then taking it without hysterics. After all, anger does not get a crowded highway to move faster. All it does is ruin your health and put you in a bad mood. So the next time your flight is cancelled or your plane can't land on time, sit back, relax, and get some work done. At least your time won't be wasted completely.

14

Hour Power at Home

Set thine house in order.

— Old Testament
Isaiah, 38:1.

Modern home life can be every bit as demanding and stressful as a high-powered career. And you probably waste as much precious time in your family life as you did on the job.

But now, you can use many of the same Hour Power techniques to save time at home as you are now using at the office. You can create the same objective activity system, use the Four D's, apply the benefits of forming goals, priorities, and using the policies of productive thinking in your home activities.

What if you could cut the time it takes to do your shopping in half? What if you could get two chores done in the time it used to take to do one? What if you could create a division of household labor that spread the family chores and errands equally among all parties? How much time might you save? How much more efficiently would your home life run? How many arguments and crises could you avoid?

The Hour Power approach to organizing your family life is simple: you merely apply the very same techniques that work so well in the office to your home activities. Let's see exactly how this works.

First, remind yourself of the emotional goal you set way back at the beginning of this book. If you are like most of the people I advise, your emotional goal had something to do with a happy family life. You had in mind to be a good parent, a loving spouse, and a helpful and guiding teacher to your family.

Based on this goal, you can begin to form priorities just as you did at work. As each new problem comes along — whether it be doing the weekly shopping, taking a child to the doctor, or painting the garage — you can return to your goal and ask yourself: "What priority does this activity have?"

I suggest that for the next few days, before you begin to implement any of my ideas into your homelife, you simply evaluate the priority of everything you do at home.

As you make this analysis, keep in mind that several factors determine homelife priorities, just as they do at work. First, there is the direct relation of a particular activity to your goals. This would seemingly place helping a child with homework above fixing a broken lamp. But many other factors can come into play. Deadlines exist at home as well as at work, and some home projects will have heavy deadlines. If your child is taking a test tomorrow, he has a deadline to make, and thus you would help him with his homework before you fix that lamp. But let's say it wasn't the lamp, but rather a window that is broken. Now imagine it begins to rain cats and dogs. Suddenly, fixing the window is more important than your child's homework, at least for the moment. This window has a higher priority.

Your home priorities are a personal matter, and I cannot give you a set of hard and fast guidelines for determining them. You must do it on your own. But for a day or two, evaluate the priority of what you are doing around the house. How many projects are really worth your time? How many could have been handled by someone else? How many could have been delayed a while longer? And how many could have been forgotten altogether?

We're back into the Four D's again, which really isn't surprising. Every human activity comes under one of the Four D's.

If you can form objective priorities that reflect your goals, you can begin to put the Four D's to work in your home. You can drop useless activities, delay those that are not pressing, give some work to other family members, and finally, do the things you must do yourself correctly.

The key is your schedule, exactly as it is at work. Trying to do housework without some kind of plan can be very inefficient. The way most of us live right now is ample proof of that fact. But with a plan — a day-to-day schedule listing exactly who will do what — you have a chance to get more things accomplished in less time around your house.

The first element of your schedule depends on how many are in your family. If you live alone, scheduling is quite simple, for whatever gets done will be done by you. If you are married with several children, however, scheduling becomes more difficult, for you must now delegate projects to the other family members.

I advise you form two schedules each week for home activities. The first list is all duties and projects to be done by the various family members from Monday through Thursday. The second schedule tells you what needs to be done from Friday to Sunday. I think it makes sense to break your schedule down in this fashion, since the tasks and business of weekends can be quite distinct from the problems of the weekdays. Chances are, you will want to schedule more work for the weekend when everyone has more free time. Of course, if you prefer to keep your weekends leisurely, you can double up during the week and do all your household jobs after a full day's work. The choice is yours, and every decision you make in scheduling reflects your personal attitudes and preferences. Above all, keep your schedule personally satisfying. If you aren't happy with your schedule, you will never follow it.

There are certain categories of housework, and you can break down your problems and duties into these groups. The first is shopping. This category includes trips to merchants for all your household needs, from food to cleaning to liquor. The second group is cooking, and it includes all aspects of food preparation. The third is cleaning, and this group should include not only sweeping and vacuuming but also household maintenance and repairs. The final group is children, and this includes all the things you must do as a parent for your children's benefit, such as helping with homework and driving them around town.

Let's say it's Sunday evening, and you are attempting to prepare a schedule from Monday through Thursday. First, examine each category and note on a piece of paper what must be done within each.

Under the first category, you may need to go to the store for food, supplies or other items. To the best of your knowledge, write down all items you can think of that you need to purchase.

In the second category, note all the meals that must be prepared within the next few days. If you can, try to plan a menu right now. The potential time and money savings from menu planning are enormous.

You should do the same things for the last two groups: cleaning and children. Whatever responsibilities you may have, write them down on your list.

With this information, you can begin to build a schedule for the next few days. But the vital thing here is that you are creating lists. Remember how much you learned about where your time, money, and energy was going from forming lists at work? You can do the same things here.

When you've got a full list of each activity, you must attempt within the coming days to evaluate it. Determine, based on your goals, which of these activities is most important, and begin to assign priorities. I'll bet that right away you can find one or two projects on that list you can drop or delay. Do this, and you've saved time already.

Now you can begin to schedule the items you cannot drop or delay. But first, you must delegate each duty that you can to a family member. I suggest you start with the children, as there will be a limit to how much they can handle. Give each child whatever job he or she can perform, and give them enough to keep them busy, but not enough to stop them from enjoying their childhood.

The remaining jobs that cannot be dropped, delayed, or delegated to a child must be done by you and your partner. The two of you are now operating as if you were one single executive, and both parties should play an active role in deciding who does what and when. The advantage of scheduling with your partner is that while you cannot order this person around like an employee, he or she also has more of a stake in the family functions and will be just as eager as you are to save time and work efficiently.

Form your schedule exactly as you would at work. Give each job a deadline, and schedule it when you have the time to get it done. Keep in mind that this schedule should not be hard and fast because many more interruptions and problems tend to arise in the relaxed atmosphere of the home than do at work.

Remember, the point here is to allow for a more flexible schedule than may be desired in the business world. What you are doing is using paper and pencil to find out where your time is going, what you must do in the days to come, and how you may be able to do it better — not to turn your home into a factory.

Perhaps this idea of making lists and schedules around the

house seems foolish to you. Many of the Hour Power techniques seem a little simplistic to people at first. But after they begin to save time and add days and weeks to their lives, most people soon change their minds. I suggest you simply try the list and schedule approach for one week. See if you aren't getting more projects done and out of the way in less time, and creating more leisure time for you and your partner.

Be sure to form a schedule that reflects the personalities of the people who share your life. I won't give you a form to use because I believe the process of scheduling homelife can be more personal, more pleasant and even more successful if you can find your own formats. Let family members make suggestions about the schedule, whether it be a criticism of your delegation of duties, or a simple comment on the format you are using. Keep time saving a family affair by keeping it personal and unique.

For a moment, let's talk about one of the biggest time consumers in your home: providing food. It involves not only shopping, storing, and cooking, but also cleaning and the exceptionally difficult task of pleasing the eater. If you have a family, you know what a chore it is to get a good meal on the table every night.

Menu planning is a tremendous time saver, but first you must accept the idea that once you commit yourself to a certain meal on a given night, you must never break your plan. Both children and adults may find this difficult from time to time, especially when they want steak and fishcakes are on the menu for tonight. But if you and your family are committed to staying with the menu, the system will save both time and money.

Let's say that on Sunday night you plan every detail of your dinners from Monday through Thursday. You now know exactly what you will prepare and consume on each of these evenings. You also know exactly what you need from the store, and you can enter these items on your shopping list. The big benefit is that you can virtually eliminate impulse shopping with a menu plan. Since you know exactly what you need, you will force yourself to purchase absolutely nothing else.

The second advantage of shopping lists is that they help you combine your errands. With the price of gasoline these days and the high value of time, you can't afford to keep running out for one or two things. Make a schedule of both food and non-food shopping lists and you'll know ahead of time exactly where you need to go. This way, you can combine two or three trips or, if you really want to save time, a full week of errands into one journey.

Another tip for shopping is never to shop when you're hungry. Numerous studies have shown that when people walk into a food store hungry, they spend a fortune. Eat before you shop, and you'll save some cash.

And a third shopping tip: leave the kids at home. Sure, it's nice to let them carry some packages. But they also tend to nag you until you buy dozens of items you don't need.

It's also a good idea to plan your shopping trips for off hours, when you won't waste valuable minutes of your leisure time standing in a checkout line.

Still one more tip: don't drive around from store to store searching for bargains. If coffee is ten cents cheaper three miles away, and your car gets 15 miles to a gallon of gas, you're better off paying the high price and skipping the trip.

Every project or job around your house should have its own list as well. Here, write down all the tools and materials you will need. This way, you can be sure that when you are ready to do that odd job in the yard, you'll have the equipment you need and won't waste time running down to the hardware store.

Generally, it's a good idea to attack one project at a time, particularly if that job has a high priority rating. And while doing this, you should look to complete each important project at home in one sitting, and try to avoid getting distracted or leaving things half done. I've discovered that one of the reasons people find household chores so aggravating is that they only get jobs done half way. For example, when trying to clean up a house or apartment, many people sweep one room, do half the dishes, and then sit down in front of the television. It took a few minutes to get ready to clean: to get the tools and materials from the closet (and several minutes to put them back again). But only about ten or fifteen minutes of work was done. Now, the person still feels a heavy pressure to do the housework, and guilt starts to accumulate. So he or she goes back, gets the materials out again, and does a little more.

Household chores can be made much, much easier if you simply attack them in one shot. If you start vacuuming, keep going until you are done. It takes more time now, but it saves stop-start time later. If you're doing the dishes, do them all and clean the sink as well. This way, they won't stare you in the face and get you upset and feeling guilty later on.

But as you do each project, keep an eye open for two- three- and four-for-ones. I've seen some women who can cook, talk on the phone, watch T.V., and shout at children at the same time. That's four-for-one, and it's a wonderful thing to see. You can begin to get this much done — all at once — all in one short time period, if you simply know WHAT you are doing, what you have left to do and exactly how you can get it done.

If your family thinks this whole idea sounds crazy, tell them more about it. Describe to them the time-saving benefits of the Hour Power techniques. And if you still don't get any cooperation, use the schedule yourself and teach by example.

Keep your schedule flexible. Leave time for unforeseen problems and all the minor crises that can occur within a family unit. Be sure your children understand that they will be rewarded for the work they do and punished for laziness — but not chastized for succumbing to natural and unpredictible problems that break into the family schedule.

When both adult members of a family work, the need for schedules and lists is greatly increased. Now that two family members are suffering from office pressures, heavy time demands, and extensive responsibilities, housework can very easily be ignored for weeks on end. The working couple should already be aware of the need for scheduling. If you're in this situation, don't wait another day to implement your objective plan for handling household affairs. You and your partner should agree to form a mutually acceptable schedule at least twice a week, and you should promise to stick to this plan and fulfill your responsibilities faithfully.

Through goals and objectives, you can begin to organize your homelife, and you may eventually find yourself reaping the same rewards here as you already are at work. Family members, just like your employees, will be more cooperative and giving. You will have a clearer idea of your responsibilities, and you'll know what projects others can handle.

In short, you will be getting more positive benefits from the time you spend with your family and loved ones in your home. You will be getting more out of your life, and giving more to the people you love and protect.

15

Personal Time

No profit grows where is no pleasure taken.

— Shakespeare
The Taming of the Shrew
Act I, scene i.

In the last few years, I've met many people who have a strange misconception of time management. They seem to think that programs like Hour Power are designed to turn men into machines, to create automatons that run on schedules like railroad trains. People who feel this way tend to know a little bit about time management — perhaps they've read a newspaper or magazine article about saving time — just enough information to form a false impression.

If time management turns you into an unfeeling robot who runs around working, achieving, and producing without taking time out for the pleasures of life, you are not following the system correctly. The point of time management is to free you . . . to give you more quality time to spend in pursuit of happiness and personal fulfillment.

So far, I have tried to share with you some tested and proven methods of saving time, both at work and at home. If you're utilizing these techniques, you should already be getting more work, more chores, and more responsibilities completed in the

197

same amount of time you used to spend achieving less. You should also be getting your work done BETTER, since you are handling projects more directly and with fewer distractions and interruptions. (Before you began using the Hour Power program, did you have more or less time to share with your friends and family?)

To a large degree, this is how many people live: their time so restricted by what they perceive as responsibilities that they overlook the emotional needs of others . . . and of themselves, as well. The fact is that several factors place demands on your personal time, and each is as important in its way as your career. The most outlandish demand on your personal time is sleep. The average person spends up to one third of his lifetime sound asleep. If you live to be 75 years old, you will probably have spent 20 or 25 years sleeping.

There are also emotional factors that demand your time. Your love life takes time, particularly if it is going well. If you're married, your spouse deserves a large portion of your personal time. Children take up a trendous amount of a parent's time and energy. And you also spend a good amount of time with your friends and relatives.

The automaton theory is not correct. The Hour Power Program will not destroy your emotional nature. Rather, it can give you more time to spend on personal needs and desires. Since you have developed methods of getting your work and chores done faster, you should now have more time — high quality time — free to share with your family and friends. When you learn how to save time, every aspect of your life can benefit.

Essentially, there are two kinds of demands on your personal time. The first are your own needs — such as relaxation, sex and sleep. Then there are the needs of others: your family and friends. The fact is, the needs of others probably come first in your life and this is only right. You are a responsible adult with many obligations. If you are married with five children, or single with a few friends, you have placed yourself in a position that involves many obligations. You OWE people your time, and you must often relegate some of your own needs to a later time and attend to your obligation NOW. Once you have satisfied the needs of others, you can begin to think about yourself.

How many other people place demands on your time? What are these demands? Can you list them? Why not get a piece of paper right now and try to list as many of the people and events that demand your personal time. List all your family members and describe some activities in which each person demands your time. Remember to include your friends and other relatives as well. These people demand your time less frequently, but still they must be considered.

When this list is complete, you can begin to see where your personal time is going. For the next evening or two, why not keep a chart of all the things you do in your personal time to fulfill the demands of others. Include in the chart any time spent with family or friends after work and after all your household responsibilities, like shopping, cooking, and cleaning, have been completed.

Your list should note what the activity was, who it was done for, and how long it took. Things like talking with your spouse, reading with a child, or having an after-work cocktail with a pal.

As the evening progresses, try to make notes of activities you could not get around to in your personal time. Maybe you cannot find the time to talk with all the people you'd like to in one evening. Maybe you skipped a dinner party to help your child with homework. Perhaps a friend called around eight o'clock and prevented you from talking with your spouse. If there is any pursuit you would have liked to have done but couldn't, due to a lack of time, note it on your chart.

At evening's end, review your chart. How much have you accomplished? How many things did you skip or sacrifice? How much of your personal time did you waste on unnecessary activities?

As you might have guessed by now, we are going to apply the Four D's to your personal time. We will look for activities you can drop, delay, or delegate in your personal life, thus freeing more time for more important and urgent matters.

The four D's cannot be applied to your personal time as easily as they were at work or with household duties. There are simply too many emotional factors involved to allow cavalier dropping, delaying and delegating. Too many people can be offended, too many feelings can be hurt. But if done with care and tact, many of the activities that now waste your personal time can be avoided.

The easiest D to apply, surprisingly, is dropping. Drop any demands on your personal time that do not bring you closer to your emotional goals. For example, don't share your valuable personal time with people who mean nothing to you. That is, don't go to a party where you won't know anyone instead of spending time with your children. This may sound obvious, but you'd be amazed how many people let this rule escape them from time to time. It seems people are always pursuing useless free-time activities and denying the needs of friends and family.

Watching television is an activity that could probably be dropped fairly easily by many people. The amount of time Americans spend watching television programs is extensive. How much time and money could be saved if each of us spent one hour less in front of the television every day? Probably about 100 million or more hours each day would be saved. Each of us could save about 365 hours in a year. That's almost 15 days, or two weeks.

Still other things can be delayed, giving you time for more

urgent pursuits. For example, that phone call from a friend at eight o'clock could have been delayed, freeing you to talk with your spouse. On the other hand, you may want to talk with your spouse later and help your child with homework right now. Whatever the exact details, delaying can be an effective way to save time while still satisfying the demands on your personal time. Delay by priority — higher priority matters come first, just as at the office. Be careful when delaying with children: they are very impatient, as every parent knows. Also, just as at work, don't delay personal matters for too long. Over-delaying is procrastination.

Delegation is a touchy matter when it comes to demands on your personal time. At work, you can have a subordinate handle a project and the results may be excellent. But family members and friends don't want the time and energy of someone else, they want you! You can't send a friend out on a date with your girl friend so you can accomplish something else.

Parents, however, are aware of the art of delegation in personal matters. You and your spouse should have a cooperative attitude toward family demands, and you can effectively delegate them to each other. For example, a child might run to his father, who may be doing the monthly bills, and asks a favor. The father will say, "Ask your mother." The child then runs to the other parent, who is able to provide the favor for the child. The child is perfectly satisfied and does not resent the father who delegated this duty. If communication is open, the two parents can share duties in this way without causing any problems between them. If both parents are going to be busy, they must decide in advance which one will handle their children's requests.

Finally, you will come to the activities you must do now. These are high priority items, things that relate to your emotional goals. Whether it be taking your lover out for dinner, teaching a child how to read, or going to a close friend's birthday party, it's something you have to do now. It cannot be dropped, delayed, or delegated. And if you have to do it, you should know how to do it right.

The first and most important step is to schedule this kind of activity for QUALITY TIME. That's a term you hear often, but you might not be sure of its meaning. For the sake of clear communication, let's agree on a definition of quality time. Simply, quality time is that time when you are free from the demands of work or household duties. All business matters are out of your mind (closure has been effected). The cooking, cleaning, and shopping are done. You are relaxed to some degree, your stomach is full, and you are ready to share yourself with someone else. Nothing else demands your attention; you are free to give yourself fully to someone you care for.

If the demand on your personal time is somewhat similar to work — for example, studying with a child — handle the project just like you would a business matter. Be direct: concentrate on the matter at hand and avoid interruptions. Look for two-, three- and four-for-one's. Can you fix a broken lamp or do some knitting while you help this child study? Can you run a quick errand while taking a child to a party? If you look for them, your personal time is probably filled with two-for-one possibilities.

Some high priority demands on your personal time can be shortened. For example, don't spend four hours at a party when two hours is enough. Talking on the phone with friends for 15 minutes is good — two hours is excessive. Look for ways to cut the amount of time you spend on these activities, and you will find yourself finding lots of time saved.

Keep in mind that when involved in high-priority personal matters, it is the sharing of time that counts. Be yourself, relax and talk. Think out loud if you feel the urge. Don't carefully form your thoughts as you might in an executive board meeting. Just relax and have fun with the people you care about.

How you spend this time is your own concern, and the result of the time you invest benefits you more than anyone else. Form your own systems, if you wish, based on the techniques I've outlined. But keep things loose and free, remain open and flexible. Look for the things that matter, and devote your time to them.

Once you have fulfilled the demands of others, it's time to make some demands of your own. Each of us has personal needs that can only be fulfilled by those we care for. If you need someone to talk to, ask your lover or friend for some of their personal time. But take note: others have their own priorities, and you may not be at the top of the list. Your friend may be very willing to give you some quality time, but not right this minute. You may find yourself being delayed. Accept this as you expect others to accept your problems and needs. Again, the key is to remain adjustable.

Your personal time also includes a certain need for solitude once in a while. The need to be alone varies in most people. Some of us require quite a bit of solitude, while others do not enjoy being on their own even for a few minutes. Like the demands you place on other people's time, solitude is a time consumer that benefits your personal needs, and it should hold a lower priority than the needs of others.

If you have the time, provide yourself with as much solitude as you feel you need. Go off alone somewhere and just relax. But what does that word relax really mean? For some people, relaxing isolation could mean working in the shop, cooking dinner, going swimming, reading . . . everyone has a different definition of relaxation and enjoyment. What you do to get away from the problems of life is a very personal choice, depending on your unique interests, desires, and needs.

But whatever you do to relax, this activity should be a major part of your personal time. More and more, relaxation is taking on a new and universal aspect: the elimination of stress and its damaging side effects. Before you can find any activity enjoyable, you must negate the nervousness and tension daily stress creates.

16

Time Technology

If you will it, the machine, this dreadful instrument of torture, will turn into a God who emancipates man for physical and mental happiness.

— Paul Lafargue

When was the last time you saw someone do a long division problem? Unless you have a school-aged child, it's a rare sight these days. And when was the last time you saw a slide rule? In less than a decade, pocket calculators have totally revolutionized the way we perform simple mathematical operations. Why have these mini-computers gained such universal acceptance so rapidly? Well, certainly accuracy is a part of it, and a lot of us would rather punch buttons than think. The essential attraction of the calculator, though, is that it saves time. You get your answer almost as soon as you key in your problem.

The calculator is just one of many new time-saving tools on the market. In fact, information processing, which includes computers, copying machines, sophisticated new telephone equipment, and a whole lot more, has become the most dynamic industry of the 1970s and 1980s. Firms like IBM, Xerox, Control Data, and Texas Instruments are prospering simply because businesses and individuals are so very concerned these days about time and productivity. I think we can learn quite a lot about ourselves by looking at some of the more remarkable breakthroughs in recent years and how they are likely to affect our lives.

To me, word processing machine are nothing short of a miracle. The first time I saw one of these incredible devices was in the offices of the *Washington Star*. A reporter types out his story on a keyboard, but there is no paper in the machine. Instead, the words appear on a small television screen. The reporter can change words, move around whole sentences and paragraphs, and add or delete sections instantly until he gets his story letter perfect. The story can then be stored in the memory banks of a giant computer until the editor is ready to review it and make any necessary changes — again everything is done electronically. Finally, the story is flashed to the typesetting room, where a machine coughs out printed copy ready to be photographed by sophisticated offset equipment. It saves time at every stage along the way.

In all sorts of office settings, word processors are coming into use. One manufacturer boasts that his machine can memorize the complete works of Shakespeare and type them out automatically at 300 words a minute. What an astonishing breakthrough this it! These computerized systems vastly increase the amount of error-free typing that a single individual can produce in a day. Word processors are still exceedingly expensive, costing about $10,000 or more. But I have no doubt that before the decade is over, the price will be in the range of every small business. The savings in man hours is incalculable.

A related breakthrough is the process called "electronic mail." It is now possible to put a letter or document in an ingenious device which converts words or pictures into electronic impulses and flashes them instantly across the nation or around the world to another similar machine which prints out a copy identical to the last detail. You can, for instance, send an exact copy of a blueprint or contract from New York to Los Angeles over the telephone wires in about five minutes. Futurists look forward to the day, not too long from now, when every home will have an electronic mail apparatus. Messages will come in at any time of the day or night and automatically be recorded for replay at your convenience. Instead of picking up your mail in the morning, you would review the messages on a video screen. An attachment could make printed copies of letters you want to keep. Or you could simply file the information away indefinitely in the memory of a home computer for recall whenever you might need it. There would be no need to physically transport letters from one place to another any longer. Think what a tremendous savings in time, labor, and energy that would mean!

Already cable television subscribers in Columbus, Ohio, and other trial markets are discovering the fabulous capabilities of the Qube system, which turns your television into a two-way communications device. One vivid display of what the Qube system can do came during the Ford-Carter debates of 1976. People with the Qube system watched the debates along with millions of other Americans. Afterwards, a major television network posed a series of questions which Qube viewers could respond to simply by pushing a series of buttons on their TV sets. "Who 'won' the debate in your opinion — Carter or Ford?" and so on. The viewers' responses were instantly tabulated by computer and the results were broadcast within a matter of minutes. It was an instant public opinion poll.

But the potential of Qube goes far greater than this. Qube viewers use their televisions to shop without leaving their homes. Merchandise is flashed onto their screens and they simply key in the code numbers of the items they want, along with the quantity, and even their credit card number, so the entire transaction can be carried out from the comfort of an easy chair. The customer saves on travel time and shopping time. One can readily imagine how the Qube system might be adapted for in-home instruction, for marketing to businesses and industries, and for town-hall-style meetings of voters to decide local issues. In every instance, electronic communications would replace travel, adding convenience and efficiency.

Time technology has even entered the kitchen. With a microwave oven you can bake a potato in five minutes instead of 50. In and of itself, this may seem like a trivial achievement, but an appliance that can save working people hundreds of hours over a period of years, freeing them for leisure and self-development, can only be regarded as a step forward.

The inventory of time-saving products could go on and on. One of the oldest and surely one of the most useful for businessmen is the dictating machine. Executives who have learned how to use these devices well — dictating letters while their secretaries are occupied with other tasks — can halve the time they spend on correspondence.

Lawyers and doctors are making increasing use of a process known as "computerized literature search." In minutes, a computer can scan through thousands of pages of legal or medical texts to find an obscure case reference or the symptoms of a rare disease.

It has always struck me that commuting was one of the biggest wastes of time in the day. What could be less productive than sitting behind the wheel of an automobile stuck in rush hour traffic? Car pooling is one response to this inefficiency. Someone still has to drive, of course, but the others in the car can use the time to read the paper, relax, or even get some work done. A technological response is the growing popularity of instructional tapes. You simply pop these cassettes into your auto tape deck, and you can learn a language, study marketing, or enjoy a best-selling novel.

Other developments of note include telephone answering machines, electronic filing systems (which take the place of those dull grey filing cabinets), automatic funds transfer which has made banking so much more convenient, those electronic paging devices or beepers that are all the fad, home computers, telephone conference call hook-ups, videotape recorders, even (in some cities) portable telephones that you can carry with you anywhere.

Don't get me wrong. I'm not advocating that you go out and buy any of these wonders. They are for the most part delightful gadgets, but for most people they are still unnecessary. The point I am trying to make here is that our technology mirrors our values. And, to the extent that this is true, it is clear that our age is concerned — one might even say obsessed — with the efficient use of time.

Ultimately, though, machines cannot solve our most fundamental time management problems. Isaac Asimov has written over 500 books without the benefit of a word processing machine (although I understand he is considering one now). William O. Douglas wrote a prodigious number of legal opinions without ever once using a computerized literature search. Conversely, it is quite possible to be hopelessly unproductive even though one is surrounded by the most sophisticated modern equipment. In the end, personal efficiency comes down to two factors: discipline and method.

These are the keys to Hour Power.

Conclusion

I've got one more exercise for you before this book ends. The idea for this came from that same Make Today Count group I mentioned in my introduction, the people who had terminal illnesses. One of the members suggested making a list of The Dumbest Things I've Done. When we started creating the list, people came up with so many endearing, charming little mistakes and faux pas that we all wound up laughing hysterically and thinking about how wonderful life really is.

The point of the exercise was to see that life is not measured simply by achievements, possessions, and dollars and cents. Life is a series of different experiences, and some of the ones that form our fondest memories are actually quite frivolous. The fact is, it doesn't matter what we do with our extra time — the time we save for ourselves. It can be something tender, or just something dumb.

The way to get the most from your time, no matter what you do, is to share the time with someone special. Show them you care, give of yourself, and be willing to accept from them.

Remember, happiness and satisfaction are two dimensional: they involve both career and social or family life. The Hour Power technique has helped you save time in your career. Use this time to improve and enjoy your home life. Andrew Marvell once said, "Had we but world enough and time . . ." Well, we do. Everyone of us has the time to live a full, happy and satisfying life. We can be productive, efficient and profitable, as well as loving, tender and exciting. It's simply a matter of balance.

In this book, we've discussed hundreds of timesavers and time wasters, and we've seen a multitude of methods and techniques to get more things done in a single day. If you can successfully implement just 20 or 30 of these ideas in your daily life, you will increase your efficiency and productivity tremendously. And the more ideas you practice, the more time you save.

Saving time — getting more from the time you have — is not a perfect science. It is growing and changing constantly. Every time I give a lecture, I have some new idea . . . some new piece of fascinating information . . . that often can re-shape many of the Hour Power theories. What you have just finished reading is the basic groundwork for a concept still in development.

You can participate in this expansion of the Hour Power Program. Experiment with new ways of saving time. Try something different now and then. Perhaps even break and exceed the rules and boundaries outlined here, just to see what happens. From now on, your life is a "field experiment" for Hour Power and time management.

Time is a wonderful gift. It is the fourth, unseen, dimension that shapes the patterns of our lives. Although some of us are given more time than others, get the most from the time you are allowed. Watch where time goes, and you can begin to direct it. Learn to save time wisely, and the force of Hour Power is yours to command forever.